D0406436

*UNDERSTANDING*

# EQUINE NUTRITION

YOUR **GUIDE** TO HORSE HEALTH
CARE AND MANAGEMENT

Copyright © 1998 The Blood-Horse, Inc.

All Rights reserved.  No part of this book may be repro-
duced in any form by any means, including photocopying,
audio recording, or any information storage or retrieval system, without the permission in writing from the copyright
holder.  Inquiries should be addressed to Publisher, The
Blood-Horse, Inc., Box 4038, Lexington, KY 40544-4038.

ISBN 0-939049-97-X

Printed in the United States of America

*UNDERSTANDING*

# EQUINE
# NUTRITION

YOUR **GUIDE** TO HORSE HEALTH
CARE AND MANAGEMENT

By Karen Briggs
*Foreword by Andrew F. Clarke,*
*BVSc, PhD, MRCVS*

The Blood-Horse, Inc. Lexington, KY

# Contents

# FOREWORD

P revention is better than cure" is an old chestnut that is currently undergoing a renaissance. This is no more evident than in the equine community where care and feeding of a family favorite or a champion stallion requires our special and often critical attention. More and more owners, trainers, and breeders are looking for practical, useful feeding information that results in improved nutritional practices. We wish to mantain not only the health of all horses but allow them to perform at the peaks of their genetic potential.

Feeds and feeding practices have far reaching effects. These can affect the reproductive efficiency of breeding stock, the development of the fetus in utero, and the young growing foal. Horses competing at all levels, from the developing athlete to the prize racehorse are the end results of the quality of a lifetime of feeding practices. And finally, the overall well-being of the mature horse in terms of day-to-day health and quality of life are determined by the quality and balance of nutritional practices.

Karen Briggs, in *Understanding Equine Nutrition*, provides solid, entry level knowledge leading to basic, practical feeding practices to achieve those goals. The great strength of this book is that it heralds the return to basics. It is a message that must be heeded at all levels of the equine industry.

The last few years have seen an abundance of new information concerning the nutrient requirements of horses and much of this is being applied in ration formulation. However, it's a major irony of modern learning that nutritional fundamentals are being overlooked and, indeed, overshadowed in the face of this new knowledge. A colorful tub of vitamins can be more attractive than having an analysis performed on the horse's feed. At the feed tub, it's not uncommon to find serious calcium and phosphorous imbalances — this is basic, established knowledge — in a ration that features a surfeit of vitamins.

In this highly readable book, the author takes a back-to-basics approach which will benefit horses of all types and ages. At present, we are at the tip of the iceberg in terms of learning more about equine nutrition. Advances in research are on the march. But this new knowledge will need to be added to the sound foundation in the core of equine nutrition, those reliable basics for all horses to benefit fully.

*Andrew F. Clarke, BVSc, PhD, MRCVS*
*chief executive officer, Equine Research Centre*
*Guelph, Ontario, Canada*

## INTRODUCTION

## *Getting Back To Simple*

**M**other Nature didn't mean for it to be so complicated. Feeding the horse, one of her most elegant creations, was supposed to be a simple thing. He and his associated equines (donkeys, asses, zebras, and a few other extinct varieties) had evolved to roam the grasslands of the world, deriving all of their nutritional needs from the tough, fibrous grasses and weeds they found there. Superbly adapted to break up stemmy plants with his large, sideways-grinding jaws and flat molars, and equipped with a digestive system ideally designed for the slow, fermentative digestion of fiber, the horse was pretty much set — all he needed was some fair-to-poor pastureland, a source of fresh water, and a natural salt lick he probably shared with many other creatures.

Left to his own devices, he wandered and grazed for 12 to 20 hours per day, those jaws methodically doing their job while his prehensile lips searched for the choicest shoots and leaves.

In the last few thousand years, the horse has found himself living a life quite different from that for which he was originally designed. Domesticated for work or for pleasure, he no longer was free to travel the grasslands and pick and choose his meals. Instead, he was more than likely housed in a box or standing stall for the convenience of his keepers, and fed at intervals that suited his masters more than his digestive tract.

Being a domesticated, stabled horse did have its perks. In the winter, instead of risking starvation when heavy snows might cover all the grazing, there was hay — dried grasses stored for just such an occasion. And there was also grain, which was offered to give the horse more energy for the work he did, and which was, frankly, delicious.

But to this day, the changes we have made to the horse's natural diet are not always in his best interest. Restricted exercise and rigid feeding schedules were never in Nature's plan for the horse. Nor was the consumption of concentrated carbohydrates. All three can be the cause of considerable digestive upset for the horse, who has not yet managed to adapt his gastrointestinal tract to our requirements.

His surprisingly small stomach (only about twice the size of a domestic pig's) is ill-equipped to handle large quantities of feed in a small timeframe, and the lack of a reverse peristalsis reflex means he can neither vomit nor burp, an evolutionary oversight which puts him at risk when the stomach is overloaded. Add to that the troubles involved with digesting concentrated, energy-rich feedstuffs he was never designed to use, and it starts to become obvious why feed-related woes like colic, developmental orthopedic disease, laminitis, and dental difficulties are so common — and so dangerous.

Somewhere along the way, feeding horses got complicated. Fear not — it CAN be made simple again. That's what *Understanding Equine Nutrtion* is about — making sense of the jargon, sorting out the ingredients, and making a plan, and a menu, that supplies all the nutrients your horse needs. Whether you have a growing yearling, a high-performance athlete, a weekend pleasure mount, a broodmom-to-be, or a dearly loved retiree, there are common-sense solutions which also will get you the best value for your feed dollar. Not to mention some peace of mind. For while we can't always duplicate Mother Nature's plan for the horse, we can certainly come up with some very viable alternatives.

# CHAPTER 1
## *What Does a Horse Need?*

It's often been observed that horses are simple creatures. And while the phrase might have been unkindly intended to describe the equine lack of intellectual complexity, it's pretty accurate when it comes to their nutritional needs.

Unlike humans with our omnivorous tastes, horses are strictly plant-eaters. Forage is the basis of the equine diet, and when the forage is of good quality and in plentiful supply, horses suffer few digestive difficulties. It's only when we deviate from the 'forage principle' that our horses run into trouble.

At first glance, however, the equine digestive tract seems to be something of an evolutionary mistake. Take the equine stomach, for example. It's surprisingly small for an animal the size of the horse — with a capacity of only about two to four gallons (or 7.5 to 15 liters). In contrast, the small intestine can reach an amazing 70 feet (about 22 meters) in length, if uncoiled and stretched out, with a diameter of three to four inches and a capacity for 10 to 12 gallons of material. Compared with what we know about other animals, the equine gastrointestinal tract seems strangely out of proportion. But from Nature's point of view, everything's just fine. In his wild state, the horse never expected to ingest large quantities of food at one sitting; his digestive system is optimally designed for his wandering, grazing lifestyle.

Let's take a slightly more thorough tour through the equine innards and see what else we can discover about the link between his physiology and his diet.

When a horse tears off a mouthful of grass with his teeth, or uses his talented lips to pick up hay or grain from the ground or a feed tub, the food is first transferred to the back of his mouth by the tongue. There, it is ground by the horse's wide, flat molars, and mixed with saliva (which almost immediately launches the digestive process by beginning to break down starches). When thoroughly chewed, a mouthful of oats will have absorbed its own weight in moisture, while a mouthful of hay will have absorbed about four times its own weight.

> ## AT A GLANCE
>
> • Forage is the basis of the equine diet.
>
> • Horses should ingest 1.5% to 3% of their body weight each day; at least half of their diet should be forage, such as hay or pasture grass.
>
> • The horse's gastrointestinal system is very sensitive; sudden changes in diet can put a horse at risk of colic.

From there, the base of the tongue pushes the food past the soft palate and into the pharynx, the opening to the eosophagus. Once in the eosophagus, a flexible tube that leads down the neck to the stomach, the food is pushed along by a series of muscular contractions. In the case of the horse, these contractions move in only one direction — meaning that what goes down, for better or worse, stays down.

Surprisingly little digestion goes on in the stomach itself. There is a small microbial population which initiates some fermentation, and there is also some enzymatic action — but because food remains in the stomach only 15 minutes, on average, before being pushed on to the small intestine, there is little time for any major food breakdown. As soon as the stomach reaches about two-thirds of its capacity, it typically starts to pass food (which, by now, is liquified) on to the small intestine, and the process continues as long as the horse keeps eating.

Although food remains in the stomach for a very brief interval, its presence (or absence) has a direct bearing on the horse's health. The upper, inner portion of the stomach's lining is made up of a non-glandular, squamous cell layer which is vulnerable to the hydrochloric acid the stomach secretes. Having food in the stomach at frequent intervals tends to absorb the acid and keep it from splashing this upper layer. Horses which are fed infrequently (one or two large meals a day, rather than several smaller meals) are more at risk of stomach ulcers, which can result from exposure to stomach acids. And it's worth noting, too, that forage does the best job of absorbing these acids. Horses fed a hay-only diet typically have a zero incidence of ulcers, while those on a mixed diet are more at risk.

The next stop on the tour is the small intestine, a coiled and convoluted tube suspended from the loin region by a fan-shaped membrane called the mesentery. The first section of the small intestine, the duodenum, is shaped like a U-turn, presumably to prevent food from being forced back into the stomach if the small intestine should become distended. The small intestine can hold up to 30% of the GI tract's total capacity, and it is the primary site for protein digestion and the absorption of amino acids (although grains are processed more thoroughly here than is forage).

Inside the small intestine, enzymes go to work to break down food materials. Starch that has not already been digested by saliva is converted to maltose, and other complex sugars and carbohydrates are broken down to simple-sugar forms so that they can be absorbed through the intestinal walls. (They then are transported by capillaries into the blood and eventually carried to the liver, the horse's major chemical processing plant.)

The small intestine is also the primary site for the digestion and absorption of fats. Most animals use gall bladder secretions to break down fats, but horses have no gall bladder. Nonetheless, horses seem able to use diets containing 10% to

15% fat very efficiently for energy and weight gain. (More on fats in an upcoming chapter.) Finally, the fat-soluble vitamins A, D, E, and K are absorbed in the small intestine, as are calcium, some phosphorus, and B vitamins. On average, it takes 60 to 90 minutes for food, now liquified, to pass through the length of the small intestine to the hindgut.

The last portion of the small intestine, the ileum, leads to the final section of the gastrointestinal tour, the hindgut, made up of the cecum, large (or ascending) colon, small colon, rectum, and anus. Here's where the bulk of the hard work of digestion is done. And rather than enzymes doing the honors, digestion in the hindgut is largely microbial — performed by a population of billions of symbiotic bacteria which efficiently break down plant fibers into simpler compounds called volatile fatty acids (VFAs), which can be absorbed through the gut wall. Not only are these bacteria a natural part of the digestive process, they're essential to it — as we'll see later when we discuss fiber digestion in more detail.

The cecum, approximately four feet long and with a capacity of seven to nine gallons, is the site of the first stage of hindgut digestion. It begins high in the horse's right flank area, and extends down and forward toward the diaphragm. Plant fibers, composed of cellulose and other hard-to-digest molecules, pass through the stomach and small intestine unaffected by enzymes, but when they hit the 'fermentation vat' of the cecum, the population of bacteria there makes short work of them, usually breaking them down in about five hours. The size and structure of the cecum (the physiological equivalent to our appendix, but far more useful) are such that it slows the passage of food in order for the microbes to do their job.

From the cecum, the partially digested food moves on to the large colon, where fermentation continues. Almost 12 feet in length, on average, and holding an impressive volume of 14 to 16 gallons, or 50 to 60 liters, of food (about 38% of the GI tract's total capacity), the large colon is also where food dwells longest — between 36 and 48 hours in total. It has a 'sacculated' construction which resembles a series of pouches. This can facilitate the breakdown of large quantities of fibrous material, but also can become a risk factor when the pouches become distended with gas during a bout of colic, as they seem custom-made for twisting and even strangulating their own tissues.

Once the food has been thoroughly processed in the large colon, it moves on to the small colon, another 10 to 12 feet long but smaller in diameter (about four inches). The vast majority of the nutrients have been absorbed by this time, and what's left in the gut is whatever the horse cannot digest or use. The main function of this portion of the hindgut is to reclaim excess moisture from the remaining material. By the time it leaves the small colon, the food has become solid again and has been molded into fecal balls. The small colon empties into the rectum, and some 36 to 72 hours after it began its journey, the waste material from a horse's meal is expelled as manure through the anus.

The equine gastrointestinal tract functions very well under normal conditions. But as every horseman knows, it's also extremely sensitive — and easy to upset. Any sudden change in diet, for example, can severely compromise the population of gut bacteria so essential for fiber digestion — and when these bacteria start dying off, the horse is at risk of colic, or at the very least, of not getting all the nutrients out of his feed. Thus it's always best if feed changes are made gradually, over a period of a couple of weeks, rather than suddenly.

Another trigger for digestive upset occurs when the horse receives a large, carbohydrate-rich meal (typically, one that is light on forage and heavy on grain). Under these conditions, the small intestine might not be able to process and absorb completely all of the nutrients before the meal moves on to the hindgut. When excess amounts of soluble carbohydrates reach the fermentation vat of the cecum, they are processed to produce not only VFAs, but also lactic acid. An increase in lactic acid lowers the overall hindgut pH level, which in turn can make the environment hostile for the gut bacteria. They begin to die off, and in the process can release endotoxins (poisons). Between these and the lactic acid itself, the stage might be set for colic or laminitis. Suddenly the old horseman's rule of feeding small amounts, often, begins to make a lot of sense, particularly if your horse is on a high-grain diet.

So, what do horses actually *need* in their diets? The basics are fresh, clean water (offered free-choice at all times except immediately after hard exercise), access to salt, and forage — lots of it. As a general rule of thumb, horses should take in between 1.5% and 3% of their own body weight in feed every day — and at least half of that (and often much more) should be forage of some kind. Whether it's pasture, hay, or some other form of roughage isn't as important as the quantity, because the horse's gut literally needs that amount in order to stay in good digestive health.

Is grain necessary? Often, the answer is no. Remember that in the wild, horses have no access to concentrated forms of carbohydrates and little need for them, because they are not doing 'work' in the sense that we humans demand. When we domesticated the horse, we asked him to expend energy over and above what he would normally do in the course of his wild day, and grains help provide the fuel he needs to perform for us. In addition, we bred horses to be larger, stronger, faster, more elegant — and often, less hardy, and more dependent on high-energy concentrates to maintain a healthy body weight. Nonetheless, grain always should be considered an optional add-on to the diet. It should be fed as necessary only to supplement the nutrition provided by the horse's forage, and in accordance with his condition, his metabolism, and the amount of work expected of him.

In the chapters to follow, we'll explore each of the ingredients of the equine diet in more detail. And we'll get a firmer grasp on how to combine those ingredients to make a healthy daily ration that provides all the essential nutrients and makes good economic sense.

# CHAPTER 2

## *Protein*

O f all the components of your horse's diet, protein is probably the most misunderstood. Long assumed to function as an energy source for the body, protein's real role is to provide amino acids (the building blocks of bones, muscles, and soft tissues) for growth and repair.

What are amino acids good for? Virtually all of the horse's vital processes, it seems. Amino acids are involved in the synthesis and the release of hormones, the synthesis of neurotransmitters and enzymes, and the regulation of sleep, appetite, and blood pressure, to name just a few functions. But primarily, amino acids are needed for the formation and repair of muscle tissue and other soft tissues throughout the body. On a fat-free, moisture-free basis, they account for approximately 80% of a horse's total structure.

Growing horses, who are 'building' new tissues as they mature, and horses being used for breeding, have a higher protein requirement than do mature horses being used for pleasure or performance. Whether working or idle, most mature horses need a surprisingly small amount of protein.

### INSIDE A PROTEIN MOLECULE

Proteins are "chains" made up of various combinations of the 22 different amino acids that exist in nature. Amino acids are relatively simple organic compounds, consisting of a basic amino group (described in chemical shorthand as COOH) and an acidic carboxyl group. Carbohydrates and fats also contain carbon atoms with hydrogen and oxygen atoms attached, but amino acids alone contain nitrogen and sometimes sulfur. The position and number of the amino acids in a single protein make up its "amino acid profile."

> ## AT A GLANCE
>
> • Protein provides amino acids, which are necessary for growth and repair of body tissues.
>
> • Contrary to popular belief, protein is a poor energy source.
>
> • A value of 0.60 grams of digestible protein per kilogram of body weight per day is appropriate for most adult horses.
>
> • Many feed manufacturers add a high-quality supplement to their balanced feeds.

When a horse ingests protein, the chain of amino acids is broken up in the digestive tract by enzymes and acids, and the individual amino acids are absorbed through the wall of the small intestine and into the bloodstream via the liver. From there, they travel to the sites where they are most needed for growth or repair of tissues.

Although amino acids are absorbed from the small intestine in a format relatively unchanged from their original chemical composition, the horse's body does have the ability to change some amino acids into different formats as the need exists, a process which occurs in the liver. However, the body does not have the ability to create all the amino acids it needs. Some amino acids can only be synthesized by micro-organisms or green plants. These are called the "essential" amino acids, and the horse must obtain them from his environment. ("Non-essential" amino acids are those the horse can synthesize himself.)

A good quality protein source is a food which provides a sufficient amount of these essential amino acids, particularly the amino acids lysine and methionine. Lysine is often called the "first limiting" amino acid — meaning that if insufficient quantities of lysine are present, then the horse's body will have difficulty using any of the other amino acids available. Methionine is second in line.

The amino acid profile of a feed is more important to a young, growing horse than to a mature one; adult horses are far less sensitive to differences in protein quality. Nor does it matter to the horse whether a particular amino acid comes from a natural source or whether it is chemically synthesized. Lysine and methionine are two essential amino acids that are often deficient in horse feeds, and since they can be synthesized inexpensively, it's quite routine for feed companies to add these ingredients to improve the overall amino acid profile biochemically. (Not all amino acids can be easily synthesized, however.)

Can protein serve as an energy source? Well, yes, but metabolically, it's an expensive process, producing three to six times more heat than the breakdown of carbohydrates or fats, and yielding considerably less energy. The heating factor might be beneficial in a cold environment, but it also might contribute to excessive sweating and possible heat exhaustion during hard work, especially in a warmer climate. And because protein is one of the more expensive ingredients in a feed, it's impractical to feed higher levels of protein in search of a performance advantage. You'll do far better by upping the levels of carbohydrates and fats — which we'll talk about in chapters four and five.

## ASSESSING PROTEIN LEVELS

Most of us determine a feed's protein level by looking at the percentage value on the feed tag under "crude protein." But the crude protein numbers can be deceptive. They do not really reflect either the overall quality of the protein (which can only be determined by the amino acid profile), or the amount of protein from that feed that the horse can digest and use. The crude protein (CP) value is based on the overall nitrogen content of a feed, and not all of the nitrogen in a feed sample is necessarily protein-bound. Nitrogen also can be found in purines, creatinine, ammonium salts, and nucleic acids, all of which might be in a feed sample. In cattle feeds, a common non-protein source of nitrogen is urea, which is added to help cattle synthesize their own proteins when the nitrogen is made available in their guts. Urea also can be found in some horse feeds, but horses are not equipped to use it the way cattle are. It does no harm, but also has no benefit.

Feed companies calculate the crude protein value of a feed based on a chemical analysis of the overall nitrogen content of a feed. Based on the idea that most proteins contain about 16% nitrogen, plus or minus 2%, the nitrogen content of a feed is divided by 0.16 (or multiplied by 6.25 for the same result) to arrive at the crude protein value. For example, if you know a feed has a nitrogen content of 1.6%, the crude protein of that product would be 10%.

The possibility of non-protein-bound nitrogen sources in the feed is what makes the CP level an estimate, at best, of what the horse actually can digest and use. As a rule, you can estimate that most grain products are somewhere between 2% to 5% lower in digestible protein (DP) than the CP numbers indicate. A product which is described as being 14% crude protein probably would deliver 9% to 12% DP. The difference is more dramatic with hay. Depending on the stage of bloom in which it was cut, sometimes only about 50% of the protein in hay might be digestible.

The availability of amino acids in a grain ration can be adversely affected by denaturing or oxidation as a result of long storage (particularly in warm conditions or bright sunlight) or improper heating (as can sometimes occur during a pelleting or extruding process). Inadequate drying of a heated feed, prior to storage, also can reduce the protein digestibility. Some feed companies anticipate these problems with feeds which undergo heat processing, and add supplemental levels of lysine (and sometimes other amino acids as well) to compensate.

## EXCESSES AND DEFICIENCIES

Horses which receive inadequate amounts of protein in their diets can suffer a number of ill effects, including decreased growth and development in youngsters, and reduced appetite, body tissue loss, slow hoof growth, energy deficit, and a poor hair coat with reduced shedding in adults. Muscle deterioration, especially in the large muscle groups of the hindquarters, also might be evident, and some horses will begin eating manure. The reduced food intake of a depressed, protein-deficient horse can become a vicious cycle, as it makes it difficult to correct the condition with a proper

**Poor pasture can contribute to protein deficiency, although the condition is uncommon.**

diet. But the protein requirements of an adult horse are low enough that true protein deficiencies are quite rare. They usually occur only when a horse is on very poor pasture or hay with no other supplemental feed, for a prolonged period of time. With a corrected diet, most of the signs of protein deficiency in adult horses can be turned around in as little as a week. The damage done to a young, growing horse, however, can be more serious.

More common, and equally damaging, is an excess of protein in the diet, especially in mature horses who have been fed by owners laboring under the misunderstanding that protein equals energy. Here's what happens: protein which is not used immediately by the horse's system is broken down to release the nitrogen atoms (the rest of the molecule being stored), and those nitrogen atoms become bound up as ammonia and urea molecules. The ammonia and urea eventually are excreted in the urine, which leads to increased water intake, increased urination, and a noticeably strong ammonia smell in the stall. And before ammonia and urea can be excreted in the urine, they must be filtered out of the blood — which, over time, can tax the kidneys. It's conceivable that this eventually might lead to decreased renal function, and that then the unfiltered urea and ammonia in the bloodstream can exacerbate liver and kidney disease.

Decreased athletic performance is another possible outcome of a high-protein diet. And in addition to all this, there's some evidence that excess protein can interfere with calcium absorption. Researchers do differ, however, on how much damage a high-protein diet can cause, and how long a horse must be fed such a diet before the effects (if any) are noticeable. There is stronger evidence for the detrimental effect of excess protein in growing horses — in one study, weanlings and yearlings fed a diet 25% higher in protein than normal suffered slower rates of growth overall and a higher incidence of developmental bone and joint problems

## HOW MUCH IS ENOUGH?

So what is an appropriate level of protein for your horse? Continuing research is changing that answer all the time, but there are some general guidelines. The amount of crude protein needed in the diet depends on the needs of the individual horse (the most pivotal question being, is he still growing?), the digestibility of the protein, and the amount of the diet consumed. As a rule, though, a value of 0.60 g of digestible protein per kilogram of body weight per day is appropriate for most adult horses.

Broodmares in their first eight months of gestation don't really need supplemental levels of protein, but in their last trimester, when the fetus does 60% to 65% of its growing, their protein requirements increase. Lactation (nursing) also demands higher protein levels; the protein content of mare's milk is highest right after foaling, and decreases gradually as the lactation period progresses. After three months of nursing, most mares are producing fairly small amounts of milk — and foals are starting to eat more solid food. At this point, a return to regular protein levels is appropriate for most mares.

Some researchers feel that stallions, in the breeding season, also can benefit from a higher level of dietary protein, which is scaled back once breeding is finished for the year.

And hard exercise (such as racing, three-day eventing, or endurance racing) does increase the need of adult horses for protein in the diet, to support increased muscle development and mass, and to replace nitrogen lost in sweat. But the overall increase is quite small — just 1% to 2%.

Which feeds provide the best protein? Interestingly, animal sources, such as milk and egg protein, and even fish and meat meal, offer the best amino acid profile and the highest levels of lysine. Milk protein is often used as the primary protein source for foal feeds, but because it is quite expensive (and because adult horses are far less sensitive to protein quality differences), it's rarely found in feeds for mature animals.

Among the plant sources, soybean and canola meal are the next best thing — they are the only two plant protein products which contain adequate amounts of lysine and methionine. Other common protein sources, such as linseed meal and cottonseed meal, have poor amino acid profiles, and are generally supplemented with amino acids added by the feed manufacturer. Grains themselves (such as oats, corn, and barley) can contain between 8% and 20% protein, but it's of poor quality — which is why most feed companies add a higher-quality protein supplement to their "balanced" feeds (sweetfeeds, pellets, and other pre-mixed rations). If the manufacturers have done their job, the feed should contain at least 0.65% lysine (on a dry matter basis). If this level isn't present, more feed will be required to get the same results (particularly with young, growing horses).

Protein, while a crucial part of your horse's diet, has to be viewed in the proper perspective — as just one part of a working whole in the nutrition scheme. Now let's examine the inner workings of fiber.

## Dietary Protein Requirements of Horses

| Class of Horse | Crude Protein (%) Recommended in Diet |
|---|---|
| Nursing foal, 2-4 months, (needs above milk) | 16 |
| Weanling at 4 months | 14.5 |
| Weanling at 6 months | 14.5 |
| Yearling (12 months) | 12.5 |
| Long yearling (18 months) | 12 |
| Two-year-old (24 months) | 11 |
| Mature horse - maintenance (idle) | 8 |
| Mature horse in light work (i.e., pleasure riding) | 10 |
| Mature horse in moderate work (i.e., jumping, cutting, ranch work) | 10.5 |
| Mature horse in intense work (i.e., racing, polo, endurance) | 11.5 |
| Stallion in breeding season | 10 |
| Pregnant mare, first 9 months | 8 |
| Pregnant mare, 9th and 10th months | 10 |
| Pregnant mare, 11th month | 11 |
| Nursing mare, first three months | 13 |
| Nursing mare, from third month on | 11 |

# CHAPTER 3

## *Fiber*

Grazing is a full-time job for horses. Given their druthers, they graze for 12 hours or more every day, their broad, flat teeth and sideways chewing motions making short work of the tough, stemmy grasses and weeds they favor. Like all true herbivores, horses get most of their daily energy requirements from eating plant fibers.

While we often provide grain and supplemental fats to our domestic horses to give them the energy to do hard work, it's important to remember that it's fiber that horses were meant to use as fuel — and fiber remains the first and most important ingredient in every equine diet. It provides all the energy horses need for everyday maintenance metabolism: ordinary functions like breathing, walking, grazing, and sleeping. Without adequate fiber, the horse's digestive system doesn't function properly — it loses the ability to move food particles efficiently through the gut, and its ability to conserve water and electrolytes also is compromised. Without fiber in the system, high-carbohydrate feeds tend to "pack" in the gut as well. The result is a horse at risk for dehydration, colic, and laminitis (not to mention stable vices like cribbing and wood chewing, which often develop when a horse's fundamental urge to chew is not satisfied).

Except in the most strenuous circumstances (such as 2-

year-olds in heavy race training), fiber should always make up at least 50% (by weight) of your horse's daily diet. And for the vast majority of adult horses, that percentage can be pushed up considerably higher — even to 100%, if the horse is an easy keeper and/or not being asked to do work. The basic principle is this: grain is an optional part of a horse's diet; roughage (fiber) is not.

Yet, ironically, horses can't digest fiber. In fact, no animal can digest fiber on its own. Animals don't produce the enzymes needed to break the beta bonds of polysaccharide fibers and make the nutrients within available for use. Fortunately, horses, like most other animals, have thousands of invisible allies — a population of intestinal bacteria, resident in the cecum and colon, which are specially adapted to digest the fiber that horses cannot digest. Through a fermentation process, these gut flora produce the necessary enzymes to convert fiber to volatile fatty acids (VFAs), which the horse can absorb. Not only do the bacteria benefit (making this a truly symbiotic relationship), but the VFAs they create provide between 30% and 70% of the horse's total digestible energy needs.

> ## AT A GLANCE
>
> • Fiber is the most important ingredient of the equine diet.
>
> • Fiber should make up at least 50%, by weight, of a horse's daily diet.
>
> • Pasture grass and hay are the most common sources of fiber.
>
> • Sugar beet pulp is also a good source of fiber.
>
> • Fiber content in pastures can fluctuate according to climate, time of year, and soil quality.

## ASSESSING FIBER QUALITY

Not all fiber is created equal. Depending on its origins, it can vary widely in terms of quality and digestibility.

Fiber consists of three main substances: cellulose, hemicellulose, and lignin. Lignin is considered 100% indigestible by either horses or the bacteria they harbor in their digestive tracts. It's the very tough stuff that gives plant material its rigidity. (Oak trees are high in lignin; tender young grass shoots are low.) But cellulose, and to a certain extent hemi-cellulose, are digestible, and it's from these two that horses derive most of their digestible energy requirements.

Cellulose and hemicellulose are polysaccharide molecules, fairly complex chemical arrangements which need to be broken into smaller units in order to be absorbed through the gut wall. Breaking the 'beta bonds' that hold the individual monosaccharide molecules together allows their conversion to VFAs. Cellulose and hemicellulose, which stem from the non-seed and non-fruit portions of a plant, such as the leaves, stems, and hulls, also are known as insoluble fiber. Soluble fiber (which makes up a relatively minor portion of the fiber in a horse's diet) is fiber stemming from the "liquid" portions of a plant: the resin, sap, pectins, and mucilages.

All plant-eaters use nearly all of the soluble fiber they ingest. But the degree of insoluble fiber that horses use varies. The sooner the bacteria go to work breaking the beta bonds, the greater the percentage of the fiber used by the horse, but even insoluble fiber which is not digested has its place in the equine diet. It helps maintain gut motility and function, as well as prevent the too-quick consumption of carbohydrates, which are readily digested and sometimes can cause digestive upset if not "cushioned" by the presence of fiber in the colon.

In practice, it's not terribly important to know how much of the fiber provided by a plant is soluble and how much is insoluble. An enzymatic test does exist, but it's rarely used because the differences are not significant from a feeding point of view. There are, however, a few ways of defining the fiber content of a feed — each with its own pros and cons.

"Crude fiber" is the value most of us are used to seeing on our feed labels or tags. It's an estimate of the total fiber in a feed, but it's not terribly accurate. The calculation that results in a crude fiber value tends to overestimate the non-fiber, car-bohydrate content of a feed, and underestimate the cellulose portion. This also leads to an overall overestimation of the feeds' caloric content and thus its feeding value. The CF is a useful approximation, but not much more.

Another value commonly used to express the fiber content of a feed is the NDF, or neutral detergent fiber. Unlike the CF, an NDF value includes almost all of the cellulose in a feed sample, and more than 50% of the hemicellulose, but it also erroneously includes a high percentage of digestible starches in its calculations. Acid detergent fiber, or ADF, generally is considered the most accurate way of expressing fiber percentages. ADF removes starches from consideration, but also removes most of the hemicellulose — and because most of the hemicellulose in a feed is used by the horse, ADF analysis, which ends up being a measure of the cellulose plus the lignin, results in an underestimation of the feed's insoluble fiber content and an overestimation of its energy content and feeding value. Nonetheless, it's the best available indicator of fiber digestibility.

CF, ADF, and NDF values all can be generated by doing a lab analysis of your feed, a service provided by most feed companies and many universities. (More about how to take a representative sample in a moment.)

## FINDING FIBER

By far the most common fiber sources for equines, of course, are pasture grasses and hay (dried grasses and legumes). For the vast majority of horses around the world, these are the sources where they get their all-important fiber fix, and rightly so, because these plants are precisely what horses have evolved to eat.

The fiber content of pasture

**Pasture grass, a common source of fiber.**

and hay can fluctuate according to the environment, time of year, soil, and stage of growth of the plants. Early spring pasture, with its tender young grass shoots, tends to be high in soluble fiber and low in lignin. Later in the summer, the grasses are tougher and less "rich." Likewise, hay cut early in its growth cycle, before it has developed seedheads, tends to be lower in overall fiber than hay cut late; but early-cut hay also is lower in lignin and higher in digestible fiber, proportionately, than late-cut. Once the plants have gone to seed, their stems tend to become tough and fibrous, and the palatability and digestibility plummet.

By contrast, the fiber content of most grains doesn't vary a

Analyzing hay can be valuable.

lot. Regardless of the stage of growth of the plant, you can pretty much depend on the fiber values of grains to be within the ranges listed in the chart on page 33. As a result, most horse owners can rely on the information on the feed tag and forego getting a fiber analysis of their grain ration. But doing an analysis of your hay (and/or pasture) can be valuable, especially as similar-looking batches of hay can be remarkably dissimilar in terms of fiber content.

The best way to take a sample of your hay is to use a tool that can take a core sample of several bales (ask your local feed store to loan you theirs). Insert the corer diagonally along the long axis of each of the bales rather than straight through the center, and take samples from at least 20 bales, ideally, mixing them together in a clean paper or plastic bag. If you don't have access to a corer, you also can get good results by doing a "grab sample," taking a handful of hay from 20 bales from different parts of the hay field and taking care to get some from the center flakes and some from the ends to get a real mixture. The proportion of leaves to stems can make a big difference to the resultant ADF and NDF values, so make sure that you have not grabbed too much of one and not enough of another. Most labs can return results within a week or two, at a cost of approximately $20 to $40.

If you want to get a fiber analysis of your pasture, a bit of observation is called for first. There is no point in analyzing the fiber content of plants your horses don't eat, so begin by watching them to see which plants are favored. Then take handfuls of only those plants from several locations throughout your field.

How do you interpret the results? As a rough guideline, forage with an acid detergent fiber value of more than 35% is considered of poor quality, and probably is past bloom. Its digestibility will be low — which is not to say that it cannot be fed, but that you will have to feed considerably more of it in order for your horses to extract the same quantity of nutrients from it that they could glean from a "younger" forage. (It's interesting to note that donkeys, which are adapted to living in harsh conditions, are considerably more efficient at extracting nutrients from poor-quality, highly indigestible forages than are horses and ponies.) ADF is considered a good overall parameter for assessing the maturity of forages.

Hay and pasture grasses are not the only fiber sources available to horses. One of the most popular alternatives is sugar beet pulp, a feed additive made from the fibrous portion of the sugar beet after the sugar has been extracted. Available in North America almost exclusively in a dehydrated format (either shredded or in pellet form), beet pulp can be rehydrated by soaking it in water for a few hours before feeding. (A recent study has determined that soaking beet pulp, traditionally thought to avert the major digestive upset that would occur when the dehydrated product hit the liquid contents of the stomach and suddenly expanded, is not actually necessary. Horses fed varying quantities of dehydrated, unsoaked beet pulp demonstrated no ill effects — though many horsemen prefer to continue soaking beet pulp in the name of 'better safe than sorry.')

Beet pulp has an ADF value of less than 28%, making it a very digestible fiber source and a useful supplement to hay or pasture for any of several circumstances. When soaked, its soft texture is easy to chew, making it a good choice for older horses, or any animal with a dental problem. It also is favored for putting weight on "hard keepers," and it makes a convenient place to hide oral medications. Many horsepeople also serve it warm on cold winter nights, though one suspects that the comforting effect of such a meal does more for the owner than for the horse! Because the crude protein content of beet pulp is fairly low (averaging around 8%), it is appropriate for almost every type of horse. It is also fairly high in calcium.

**Bran is not the best fiber supplement.**

Bran, another traditional way of supplementing fiber, is a less suitable choice. Bran is the outer layer of the grain kernel which is removed in the process of milling. Wheat bran is the type most commonly fed to horses (though rice bran is sometimes used as a fat supplement in small quantities). A fluffy, low-density feed, bran is only half as dense as (and thus delivers only half the digestible energy of) oats, and only a quarter as dense, and energy-rich, as corn or barley — so despite its ADF of approximately 15%, it takes a lot of bran to provide sufficient fiber for the average adult horse. Furthermore, its purported laxative effect has been shown to be a myth. Whether fed dry or wet, bran has no demonstrated "loosening" or "regulating" effect on the bowel. (The loose manure many owners observe after the feeding of a weekly bran mash is, in fact, the result of a mild digestive upset from a sudden change in the diet!) An occasional small bran mash probably does no harm, but as a fiber supplement, there are better choices. If you must feed it, make bran no more than 10% of your horse's total ration.

Two other fiber supplements are lignin-rich and largely indigestible. They are added to the diet mostly as "busy food" — useful in keeping obese or idle horses chewing away — and to some extent, to aid in digestive health by keeping gut motility up to speed. Chaff (chopped straw or low-quality hay) is a feed additive often used in the United Kingdom, mixed in with the grain to slow down a horse who bolts his feed, "fake out" an overweight or greedy horse who would like to be getting more grain than he needs, or "cushion" the system of a horse with a tendency to colic. Oat straw and barley straw are commonly used to make chaff, and while their ADF values are usually more than 35%, they are certainly harmless, even if they provide more bulk than nutrition to the diet.

Grain hulls are another inexpensive way to provide that same effect. High in crude fiber (up to 50% higher than grass hay) and low in energy, hulls can be used to replace some or all of the forage in a horse's diet. The hulls of most cereal grains can be safely fed to horses. Oat hulls are particularly popular, and coarsely ground corn cobs are another similar product. There is one caveat: Because hulls are often ground, they tend to be dusty. Blending them with a little water or molasses can help keep the dust down, or you can buy a pelleted version.

One downside to most of these alternate fiber sources is that they are consumed by the horse far faster than he can consume hay — so any time you substitute another fiber source for forage or pasture, you could be giving your horse less opportunity to satisfy his compelling urge to chew (which is part and parcel of his herbivorous nature). Boredom can translate that urge into stable vices, co-prophagy (eating manure), even munching on the stall walls or his neighbor's tail.

Feeding small meals, often (at least three to four times a day) is a partial solution. But under most circumstances, forage is still the best and most natural choice for most horses. Other fiber sources can be used as supplements to hay or pasture, or as a complete substitute only in cases like advanced respiratory disease (such as heaves), or dental problems that make it impossible for the horse to chew and process forage.

For more on hay, take a look at chapter 7.

## Representative Fiber Values for Common Horse Feeds

| Feed | Crude Fiber (%) | Acid Detergent Fiber (ADF) (%) |
|------|-----------------|-------------------------------|
| Alfalfa, early hay | 23 | 32 |
| Alfalfa, late hay | 30 | 39 |
| Barley | 6 | 6 |
| Beet pulp | 20 | 27.5 |
| Bran, rice | 13 | 20 |
| Bran, wheat | 10-12 | 13-15 |
| Clover hay | 21-31 | 32-36 |
| Corn | 2.5 | 4 |
| Corn cobs, ground | 35 | 40 |
| Grass hay, early | 31-34 | 35-41 |
| Grass hay, late | 31-35 | 38-45 |
| Molasses | 0-0.5 | 0 |
| Oats | 11-12 | 16 |
| Oat hay | 32 | 38 |
| Oat hulls | 33-36 | 40-44 |
| Sorghum | 2.8 | 9.3 |

# CHAPTER 4

## Energy and Carbohydrates

If forages provide the "maintenance" energy horses need for the workings of everyday life — grazing, sleeping, wandering from pasture to pasture, maintaining internal temperature — then consider cereal grains the turbo-charged portion of the diet. Their main function is to provide higher concentrations of energy, in the form of carbohydrates and starches, so that the horse can do the work we ask of him.

The amount of energy your horse needs rises in direct proportion to how fast, how long, and how hard you expect him to perform. At the lowest end of the spectrum are horses who are idle, or perhaps work only a few times a week at a very slow pace. Most pleasure horses and school horses fall into this category. At the other end are racehorses, who probably work harder than any other category of equine athlete (particularly because they're often asked for peak performance while they're still physically immature). And somewhere in between might be your equine athlete — whether he's a Western pleasure horse, a Grand Prix jumper, a polo pony, or one of a four-in-hand driving team. His energy requirements will more than likely not be completely met by hay or pasture alone.

Work isn't the only thing that can raise a horse's energy requirements above the maintenance level. Environmental conditions, his physical fitness, and his degree of fatigue all play a role. Even when all of these factors are identical, individuals can vary in their energy needs. We all know of high-strung horses who are "hard keepers," and their metabolic opposites, the easy-going types who maintain weight easily even in hard work. Breed type and temperament both have a role to play here.

Pregnancy also places increased energy demands on the mare, though only in the last three months of gestation, when the fetus is developing most rapidly. Lactation and growth are two other situations in which energy needs are higher than usual. Even size can have

**Pregnant mares have higher energy needs.**

something to do with it. Recent studies have indicated that the energy requirement of horses at rest is proportional to the horse's bodyweight — so in theory, the energy requirement of a 500-pound pony is about half that of a 1,000-pound horse.

> ## AT A GLANCE
>
> • Carbohydrates and starches provide higher concentrations of energy.
>
> • Grains are the most convenient source of carbohydrates and starches.
>
> • Energy needs depend on the level at which a horse is working.
>
> • Environmental factors and a horse's physical fitness level also play a role in a horse's energy requirements.

## UNLOCKING THE ENERGY

Carbohydrates and starches, contained in grains, are the most convenient way to provide extra energy to your horse. A carbohydrate molecule is composed of simple sugars (also called monosaccharides) such as fructose, glucose, galactose, and xylose. Many glucose molecules, attached together by "alpha bonds," form the polysaccharides called starch (which is present in plants), and glycogen (present in animals). These two are sometimes called soluble or non-fiber carbohydrates, and both are readily used by the horse, providing much of his dietary energy. But other forms of carbohydrates contribute a substantial amount of "juice" as well. As we saw in the previous chapter, glucose molecules which are attached together by "beta bonds" instead of alpha bonds, form the polysaccharide cellulose (insoluble fiber). Likewise, hemicellulose is constructed of many molecules of the monosaccharide xylose, connected by beta bonds. So while we consider fiber and carbohydrates to be two different things, they are really very closely related.

Monosaccharides are the only form of carbohydrate that can be absorbed from the intestinal tract, so the alpha or beta bonds of polysaccharides must be broken down in the gut before the horse can begin to use (or store) the simple sugars. The digestive enzyme amylase is responsible for this important job. It is secreted by all animals, primarily from the pancreas, into the small intestine. Amylase takes care of the first step of carbohydrate digestion, breaking the polysaccharide molecules down into a disaccharide (a two-sugar molecule) called maltose. After that, the disaccharide enzyme maltase takes over to break down maltose further into its monosaccharide components. Two other digestive enzymes, lactase and sucrase, also might be called into play if lactose (milk sugar) or sucrose (table sugar) is present in the gut. (Lactase is usually present only in young, nursing horses and later becomes scarce enough that adult horses have difficulty digesting milk products, usually ending up with diarrhea.) Because these enzymes emanate from the interior intestinal wall, any damage to that area (as from enteritis, for example) results in impaired carbohydrate utilization. Large amounts of carbohydrates can remain in the gut, again causing diarrhea.

The simple sugars that pass through the intestinal wall are

almost immediately available for energy use by the horse. Often, however, the energy isn't needed right at that moment, so the body busily begins re-assembling the sugars in the form of glycogen, so that they can be stored. Storage depots in the kidneys, liver, and muscles give the horse a substantial energy warehouse, and if they become full, any extra monosaccharides are then converted to and stored as fat. Both glycogen and fat can be drawn on for energy whenever they're needed (more on fats in the next chapter). The hormone insulin acts as a glucose regulator in the bloodstream, determining how much sugar remains there and how much gets stored away.

## DETERMINING DIETARY ENERGY

Not all the energy contained in a feed is accessible to the horse. A significant portion of it is lost in the conversion process of digestion. The Digestible Energy (DE) is the value most often used to describe the usable portion of the total energy, or Gross Energy. It consists of the portion of energy NOT lost in the feces. However, like many things in the nutritional world, it isn't perfect: the DE value doesn't take into account energy lost in urine (and to a lesser extent, in gastrointestinal gases such as methane), nor energy lost as heat in the actual digestion and absorption of the food. Nonetheless, DE values for foods are far easier to come by than values which do take these minor factors into account (which are far more difficult to calculate), so DE is the unit in common usage. Just keep in mind, when you see a DE value, that it's likely to be a little generous.

Another way of calculating the energy content of feeds is by the familiar Calorie, the amount of heat generated by oxidation (burning) to raise the temperature of a kilogram of water by one degree Celsius. (The capital-C calorie is actually shorthand for a kilocalorie; the original small-c calorie unit is the amount of heat required to raise the temperature of one gram of water one degree. It's too small a unit to be of practical use when discussing nutrition.) When dealing with horses and other large animals, nutritionists usually switch to the Megacalorie (Mcal), which is 1,000 kilocalories. It saves writing a lot of zeros.

A third unit in common use is TDN, or total digestible nutrients, a measure of digestible energy expressed in either weight or percentages. TDN is the sum of a feed's digestible carbohydrates, its digestible protein, and its digestible fats multiplied by 2.25 (because fats provide about 2.25 times more energy than carbohydrates or proteins). One kg TDN is approximately equal to 4.4 Mcal. (If you use TDN as the basis

**Light work includes Western pleasure.**

of your ration formulating, make sure you have a TDN value for horses, not ruminants, such as cattle. Ruminants are much more efficient, digestion-wise, than horses, so calculations for energy available from forages are generally 5% to 15% higher. If you formulate a ration for a horse based on ruminant TDN, you will likely be providing too little feed in the long run.)

There are a couple of formulas which can help you calculate how much digestible energy your horse needs for his daily maintenance needs (without weight change).

For the average horse weighing less than 600 kg (1,320 lbs), use this formula:

MCAL DE/DAY = 1.4 + 0.03 X (KG BODY WEIGHT)

So for example, if your Standardbred mare weighs 450 kg (that's 990 pounds), she would require 1.4 + (0.03 x 450) Mcal ... which equals 14.9 Mcal of digestible energy per day for her maintenance metabolism.

If your horses weigh more than 600 kg, they will have

lower energy needs per kilogram than smaller animals. So they have a slightly altered formula:

MCAL DE/DAY = 1.82 + (0.0383 X KG BODY WEIGHT) — [0.000015 X (KG BODY WEIGHT)$^2$]

Using this formula, a 750 kg Belgian gelding, for example, would require 1.82 + 28.73 — 8.44 = 22.11 Mcal/day.

**Three-day eventing constitutes intense work.**

You also can do rough calculations for how much additional energy your horse will need for various kinds of work. For ponies and light horses, the Mcal DE/day for light, medium, and intense work has been estimated at (respectively) 1.25, 1.5, and 2.0 times the amount needed for maintenance. What constitutes light, medium, or intense work? It depends, of course, on a number of factors, but generally speaking, light work includes such activities as Western or English pleasure, trail riding, quiet pleasure driving, and acting as a beginner level lesson horse. Medium work encompasses functions like ranch work, roping, cutting, jumping, barrel racing, and dressage; and intense work includes race training, polo, endurance riding, and upper-level three-day eventing.

Given the opportunity and the good health to do it, horses will choose to consume enough feed to meet their energy needs as a rule. Four things can contribute to a horse's not getting enough energy:

1) a sufficient quantity of food is not available;

2) his gastrointestinal tract will not hold enough of the available feed because the DE density of the feed is too low (as with poor-quality hay, for example);

3) he can't consume enough because of a physical problem (such as an injury or dental problem);

4) he doesn't want to consume the feed because illness, stress, unpalatable feed, or inadequate water intake has left him with no appetite.

Regardless of the reason, the first sign of inadequate energy intake is a depressed attitude. Eventually, hormonal changes will decrease the body's energy utilization, shutting down growth or milk production and reducing physical activity. They also will call on the system to draw on stored fats and carbohydrates, resulting in weight loss. The horse's stores of carbohydrates are depleted within the first few days of total food deprivation, and within a week, the body adapts, drawing on body fat and conserving the body protein.

But if starvation continues, the horse will have no choice but to turn to his structural protein for energy once the fat stores are depleted. First, proteins in the blood, intestines, and muscle are drawn on, with those lending structural support to bones, ligaments, tendons, and cartilage following after. By the time muscle-wasting or weakness is evident, feed-deprivation-induced changes in other body functions are already well underway. The good news is that providing adequate calories usually can reverse the damage over time.

Far more common, fortunately, with domestic horses at least, is an energy excess. Horses who routinely receive too much feed will develop increased fat stores for a start. Some of the excess energy will also be given off as heat (a mechanism used by many animals, including humans); but the horse is unique in that he also compensates for excess energy intake by increasing his physical activity. The result is familiar to many of us: a snorting, shying, bucking explosion looking for a place to happen! In the young horse, excess energy also contributes to rapid growth, which can sometimes increase the risk of developmental orthopedic (bone and joint) problems. Reducing the amount of feed, especially grains, in the diet and providing more outlets for exercise will usually take care of this problem.

## DELIVERING THE GOODS

Supplying your horse with energy-rich carbohydrates is as easy as running down to the feed store and picking up a bag of grain. Or is it? All grains do contain large amounts of carbohydrates and starches, but not all grains are equivalent. Here's what they do have in common: they are four to eight times as heavy as baled hay (per unit volume); they're low in fiber and about 50% higher in dietary energy than average-to-good quality hay; and starch makes up 55% or more of their total dry matter.

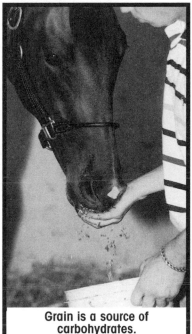

Grain is a source of carbohydrates.

Grains with seed coats, like oats, tend to be somewhat lower in carbohydrates and higher in fiber than hull-less seeds like corn, which are very carbohydrate-dense. On the whole, starch digestibility by the horse is high — researchers estimate that the average horse uses from 87% to 100% of the starch he's given. And therein lies a problem. When a grain meal hits the horse's small intestine, some of the starch is digested and absorbed as simple sugars, as it's meant to be, but the rest, instead of passing through the system undigested, is converted by the microflora in the cecum to volatile fatty acids and lactic acid. If the production of these acids is rapid enough (as can happen when a horse gets a large grain meal at one sitting — or when he breaks into the feed room and gorges), cecal acidosis can result — a condition which can trigger diarrhea, colic, and laminitis.

To reduce the risk of this reaction, it's wise to follow the old horseman's credo of "small meals, often." This gives the small intestine time to process the carbohydrates before the system moves everything along to the cecum. The more carbohydrates that get digested in the small intestine, the less cecal acidosis results. Because forage in the system can decrease the amount of grain processed in the small intestine, it's best not to feed hay for an hour or more before feeding grain, or for three or more hours afterwards — a rule that was definitely not in the old horseman's lexicon.

Other approaches which can help include giving preference to grains with fiber-rich hulls, such as oats, or choosing grains which have been processed by grinding or heat treatment to improve the digestibility of the starches. More on choosing grains in chapter 9.

## Digestible Energy Levels of Grains

| Grain | Digestible Energy (Mcal/kg) | Digestible Energy (Mcal/lb) |
|---|---|---|
| Oats (regular) | 1.3 | 2.8 |
| Oats (heavy) | 1.4 | 3.1 |
| Corn | 1.5 | 3.4 |
| Barley | 1.5 | 3.3 |
| Sorghum (milo) | 1.45 | 3.2 |
| Wheat | 1.55 | 3.4 |
| Rye | 1.53 | 3.4 |
| Ground rice (rough) | 1.55 | 3.3 |
| Millet | 1.35 | 3.0 |
| Wheat bran | 1.5 | 3.3 |
| Rice bran | 1.3 | .9 |
| Molasses | 1.6 | 3.5 |

# CHAPTER 5

## *Feeding Fats*

If there's a nutritional buzzword for the millennium, it's fat. We humans still might not understand fully the differences between saturated and unsaturated fats, let alone "good" cholesterol and "bad" cholesterol — but we all know how to count our fat grams! While we struggle to keep our diets as low-fat as possible, fat has a different focus when it comes to the horse... because it's only in recent years that we've recognized the value of *raising* the fat levels in an equine athlete's diet.

Of course, the average human diet (at least in North America) contains far more than the maximum 30% fat that's recommended for good health. The horse's natural diet, in contrast, contains almost no fat at all. Forages and fibers contribute none, and most grains fed to horses contain only between 2% and 3.5% fat overall. While this leaves the horse at low risk for cardiovascular clogging, it does mean that, traditionally, carbohydrates have been considered the obvious and "natural" energy source for performance horses, and fat has rarely been considered, beyond that little splash of corn oil that's considered good for a shiny coat. Only in the last couple of decades have we begun to realize that fat is also a valuable energy source — and one with many advantages.

High-fat diets (anything over and above the 2% to 3.5% supplied by a standard grain-plus-forage diet) provide several perks, most notably in terms of energy production for high-level equine performance. Pound for pound, fat supplies almost two and a half times as much energy as the equivalent weight of carbohydrates or starches (traditionally supplied by grains such as oats, corn, or barley). If you wish to supply more energy to your horse without significantly increasing his overall feed intake, supplementing the fat in his diet can be an excellent way to accomplish that.

## AT A GLANCE

- Fat is now recognized as a valuable energy source.

- Horses fed high-fat diets might have a performance advantage over horses on high-protein or high-carbohydrate diets.

- A fat-supplemented diet can contain up to 8% to 10% fat.

- Corn and soy oil are good sources of fat.

Fat also is easily metabolized by horses, despite the fact that their digestive systems (best adapted for the processing of fiber) didn't really evolve to deal with it. Studies have shown that as much as 20% overall fat in the diet is well tolerated by horses, with no ill effects noted. Indeed, fat might well be easier for horses to digest than carbohydrates. It has been demonstrated that a fat-supplemented diet, unlike a high-carbohydrate diet, has no effect on the pH of the cecum (and thus no detrimental effect on the beneficial microflora inhabiting the large intestine). Fat appears to be absorbed almost exclusively in the small intestine.

Another interesting fat digestion fact is that horses can use fats well despite the fact that they have no gall bladder. In most mammals, the gall bladder excretes bile and salts to help break down fats, but in horses, the liver seems to take over that function, with no fat digestion problems that research has been able to identify.

Fat-supplemented diets also have been shown to decrease the amount of energy used for heat production in the horse's body. This decreases the horse's heat load, and increases the amount of energy available for physical activity. In one study where horses ate a fat-supplemented diet, the horse's total body heat production decreased by 14%, and the diet had no effect on the amount of energy needed for maintenance metabolism, therefore leaving more energy available for performance requirements (or for energy storage in the form of glycogen or fat). The end result was that over 60% more energy was available for physical activity (regardless of the ambient temperature or how skinny or plump the horse was at the time).

Some of the most compelling research behind fat is that which demonstrates a fat-supplemented diet's benefits for high-performance horses (in sports such as three-day eventing, racing, polo, endurance racing, and cutting). But to understand how fat acts as a performance enhancer, we first have to understand some exercise physiology basics.

## DIETARY FAT FOR ATHLETIC PERFORMANCE

Grains, the "traditional" feed for high-level physical activity, are suppliers of carbohydrates and starches — versatile energy substrates which fuel the horse's muscles for athletic endeavors of all kinds. Fat is also an energy substrate, which while not as flexible as carbohydrates in terms of the types of activities it can fuel, might in many ways help the horse's body use itself more efficiently and with less fatigue.

There are two main energy pathways by which a horse's muscle cells are fueled to do work. (A third pathway, called "anaerobic alactic" metabolism, is a "start-up" system which only comes into play for bursts of hundredths of a second.) The predominant energy pathway is aerobic metabolism, which the muscles use whenever they can, for all low-intensity and endurance activities, especially those requiring a continuous effort of longer than two minutes (and possibly lasting many hours). Blood glucose, which is derived from carbohydrates and starches when they are broken down in the gut, is the main energy substrate for aerobic metabolism, and muscle cells will draw on blood glucose as needed.

Oxygen, from the lungs, is the "fuel" used to burn the glucose in order to produce ATP (adenosine triphosphate, the "energy molecule") along with the non-toxic byproducts, water and carbon dioxide.

Blood glucose levels are regulated by insulin, which responds to high blood glucose levels (as happens two to three hours after a high-carbohydrate meal) by increasing and converting excess glucose to glycogen, the form in which it is stored in muscle, fat, and liver cells. Another hormone, glucagon, can reverse the process, converting glycogen back into glucose and releas-ing it into the blood. This mechanism, while efficient, is not fool-proof — sometimes insulin might "spike" in response to a large load of carbohydrates being introduced, causing large amounts of blood glucose to be convert-ed to glycogen and stored away. This can leave a horse hypo-glycemic (low in blood sugar) and feeling weak and fatigued.

Sprint activities like pole bending are fueled by anaerobic metabolism.

As long as a horse stays below a certain performance threshold (which can vary somewhat depending on the horse's activity, his conformation and muscle bulk, and his degree of fitness), he can work aerobically. It's essentially a "clean-burning" system which horses can maintain indefinite-ly, as long as fuel continues to come in on a regular basis. Thus it's the least taxing to the system — but as blood glucose drops, and then glycogen is drawn upon, and then depleted, fatigue can set in, and force the horse's body to switch to another energy pathway.

During high-intensity exercise of short duration, or when glycogen depletion no longer allows a horse to work aerobically, his muscles will use anaerobic lactic metabolism. "Sprint" type activities of about 10 seconds to two minutes in length are typical "anaerobic" activities; barrel racing is a good example. When the aerobic system is working close to its full capacity, the anaerobic system also will "kick in" like a supercharger, augmenting rather than replacing the aerobic metabolism.

The anaerobic lactic system is entirely dependent on stored glycogen in the muscles as an energy source. It is a far less efficient system than aerobic metabolism in terms of the ATP produced per molecule of glycogen, and so it depletes glycogen rapidly. It also has a toxic byproduct, lactic acid, which is the payoff for that sudden burst of energy. Lactic acid is usually swept away from the muscles by the bloodstream, but if a horse is exercising at high intensity, the rate of production might exceed the rate of removal, allowing lactic acid buildup in the muscles. The point at which lactic acid begins to build up is called the anaerobic threshold (occurring at a heart-rate of 140 to 150 beats per minute), and it's a major contributor to fatigue and subsequent performance reduction. In the short term, lactic acid accumulation lowers the pH within the muscles, inhibiting enzyme action. In the longer term, it can damage muscle fibers and create muscle stiffness that develops after exercise.

Pushing back that anaerobic threshold is a major focus of performance enhancement, and that's where fat (finally!) comes in. When fat is broken down in the digestive tract, it becomes fatty acids — which can fuel aerobic metabolism, but not anaerobic. Adding fat to the diet provides a second source with which the body can continue to work aerobically, delaying the switchover to anaerobic metabolism, and thus postponing lactic acid buildup, fatigue, and performance· deficits.

Studies have indicated that if the horse's system has supplemental levels of fat available as an energy source, it can "learn" to use it in preference to glycogen, thus increasing the amount of muscle glycogen the horse maintains. Horses fed a high-fat diet also appear to have better muscle glycogen utilization during anaerobic (sprint-type) activities, and no change in their blood glucose concentration (and thus their insulin concentration) while working anaerobically. During aerobic (endurance-type) activity, the same horses showed less decrease in their blood glucose concentration than did horses fed a traditional grain diet, and there was muscle glycogen sparing (less utilization of stored glycogen). This glycogen sparing helps delay fatigue, an important factor in performance enhancement. As a racing sage once observed, it isn't so much which horse is going the fastest at the end of the race — it's more about which horse is slowing down the least!

Horses fed high-fat diets (15% added soy oil) appear to perform better than those fed either a high-starch diet (40%) or a high-protein (25%) diet

**High-fat diets can help horses in high-speed activities.**

for both high-speed (racing) activities, and moderate-speed activities (fast trot/slow canter speeds of about five meters a second), both in terms of the blood glucose concentration (which decreased less, and for a shorter duration), and in terms of plasma lactate (lactic acid) levels, which were substantially lower than those found in horses on high-carbohydrate diets. These benefits might produce only subtle results — but even a gain of a few feet on a racetrack might result in a Derby win. Even at lower levels of performance, the change can be valuable. For example, a low-goal polo player might find that his horse can recover more quickly, and perhaps be able to play one more chukker, than before.

That's not to say that fat is a miracle ingredient. For reasons we don't yet fully understand, the horse's body must "learn" to use fat as an energy source, a process that requires considerable metabolic adaptation on the part of the muscle cells. It can take three to four weeks, and the blood chemistry might continue to adapt for up to six weeks. What this means is that you can't just start feeding fat the day of the big race, and see results. You not only have to put your horse on the fat-supplemented diet a good month in advance, but you also have to challenge his system so that it begins to adapt. For a racehorse, that means you have to race him on the new diet, not just train him conservatively, in order to help him begin to assimilate the new energy source.

And as nice as it might be to contemplate improving further on the benefits of feeding fat by feeding greater amounts — perhaps eliminating grain altogether — unfortunately, it just doesn't work that way. Remember that only carbohydrates can fuel the anaerobic system of metabolism, which all horses use to some degree in their work — and that forages alone provide a minimum of carbohydrate. (Fed by itself, forages provide plenty of fuel for maintenance metabolism, but not enough, for the vast majority of horses, to do the work we ask of them.) Grain in the diet is an important fuel source for any performance horse, and study after study has confirmed that high-fat diets work best in conjunction with fairly high grain diets, for maximum benefit in hard-working horses (such as 100 mile endurance racers, Thoroughbred and Standardbred racehorses, and upper-level three-day-event horses).

So what level of fat is optimum for a performance benefit? That number is still under some debate. Some researchers now recommend a level of 10% (by weight) of the total daily diet for horses working at the extreme end of the athletic spectrum, though slightly lower levels (about 8%) might be more appropriate for horses working at a lower level of intensity. The level of fat you choose might depend somewhat on the activity you're asking your horse to perform. Some studies have indicated that levels up to 15% are beneficial for horses who are involved in intense, long-term endurance activities (chiefly competitive trail and endurance racing, and upper-level three-day-eventing). However, even a level of 6% to 8% will result in some performance benefit for horses involved in more moderate activity.

Feeding fat can also be well worth considering for reasons other than performance enhancement — good news for the vast majority of us, who are dealing with horses NOT at the cutting edge of high performance.

**High-fat diets can benefit older horses.**

First, it's true that supplemental levels of fat can enhance the quality and shine of the hair coat, giving your horse a healthy glow that reflects particularly well in the show ring. Supplemental fat can also help put or keep weight on a "hard keeper," provided he is not in heavy work. Just as we do (far too efficiently, sometimes!), horses will store excess fat in the adipose tissues — so for plumping up a skinny horse, added fat is an excellent solution which carries far less risk of stomach upset and other complications than does a switch to a high-carbohydrate diet.

Older horses might benefit from a high-fat diet, too. As the condition of their teeth starts to deteriorate and their digestive efficiency begins to wane, easily digested fat can help prevent them from losing condition and becoming ribby.

By the same token, broodmares can reap the rewards of added fat. Studies have indicated that a mare who has recently "gained some condition" (easily achieved by feeding added fat for a month or two before breeding) might catch more easily and maintain her pregnancy with less difficulty. In addition, a high fat diet can help her deal with the stress of lactation, which can be considerable. A third perk is that her milk will be higher in fat (mare's milk being fairly low to begin with), and as a result, her foal will tend to gain weight and condition more easily.

Fat is often touted as an ingredient that provides energy without the "hotness" that carbohydrates provide — so it is sometimes recommended in an effort to calm down a hot horse. Unfortunately, this one is a myth. As experts in both human and equine research have noted, carbohydrates are falsely accused of causing a "sugar high," and so substituting fat for a portion of the grain being fed will make no difference to a horse's temperament or attitude. The idea of horses getting "hot" from high-grain diets has more to do with their being in hard training at the same time their grain ration is increased, than it does with any physiological effects on a horse's manners. As most trainers know, when you're exercising vigorously, you feel good, and you have more energy. The fact that you're getting more groceries is coincidental.

## HOW TO FEED FAT

Adding fat to your horse's diet can be done in a number of ways. Practically any digestible source of fat, either vegetable or animal, might be used. The only source to avoid is the rumen-protectant variety of fat that is designed for cattle, which horses will find at best indigestible, and at worst, toxic. (You won't run into this one unless you ask for it specifically at the feed store.) It's interesting to note that horses actually can digest fat from animal sources (such as tallow) very well, despite their vegetarian innards. From an economic standpoint, animal-fat products are generally much less expensive than comparable vegetable fats or oils. But animal fats are seldom used in horse rations, for two reasons: First, at room temperature, they are usually solids, so they must be heated to liquid in order to mix with a grain ration; and second, their palatability is generally low (try to get a horse to eat something that smells like bacon grease!).

Of the vegetable sources of fats (which usually come in the form of oils), corn and soy oil are traditional favorites, and readily available at most feed mills as well as many supermarkets. Other vegetable oils are just as suitable, however, although many horseowners avoid canola oil as its palatability isn't as good as some of the others. Top-dressing your horse's grain ration with oil is a simple process of measuring and pouring — but like any feed additive, it should be introduced gradually, over a period of two to three weeks.

There are also other feed additives that are relatively high-fat, most notably rice bran, which have gained considerable popularity in parts of the United States. Rice bran products, which come either as a powder or as an extruded pellet, are approximately 22% fat, which means you have to feed considerably more of it to get the same benefits as you would from a 100% fat product such as vegetable oil. Rice bran has the advantage of being much more stable, however, and is often preferred in warm, humid climates where oils and animal fats tend to go rancid very quickly. Extruded soybeans, another high-fat product, are good for young growing horses because they are also a good protein source. They're not as appropriate, for that same reason, for mature animals.

One of the simplest ways to add fat to your horse's diet is to choose a commercial grain ration that is fat-supplemented. Many feed companies now offer these products, usually as part of their premium line. Fat-supplemented feeds are often equipped with extra anti-oxidants to prevent spoilage, a management perk, and have camouflaged the fats with other ingredients so there is no loss of palatability. Any feed which contains more than about 3.5% fat is considered to be fat-supplemented. Look for a crude fat level of 8% to 10% on the label (and if your horse is a mature animal not being used for breeding, a protein content of 10% to 12% at most), and introduce it gradually to your horse's diet. If your horse objects to top-dressed oil or rice bran, a fat-supplemented sweetfeed or pellet might be the best way to go.

Whatever way you decide to add fat to your horse's diet, you must consider how it will affect the overall nutrient balance of his daily ration. If you add fat to your horse's routine, but don't increase his exercise level or cut down on his grain, he's likely to get fat. However, if you cut back on your horse's grain, you also reduce the concentration of vitamins and minerals he receives. For this reason, it's important to work with an equine nutritionist (whom you can contact through your feed dealer, local veterinary college, or state extension service) to help you make the necessary adjustments so that your horse doesn't get cheated out of essential minerals, like calcium and phosphorus. You might have to consider adding a supplement to compensate for these losses.

If you're feeding a commercial ration that is a "premium" product, you might not have to worry about deficiencies of vitamins and minerals, since many of these are deliberately designed with an excess of most nutrients. And if you decide to go with an all-inclusive high-fat feed, the feed company has likely already done the ration balancing for you. Consult with your equine nutritionist to be sure.

One thing fat is not going to do is make feeding any cheaper. Pound for pound, it usually works out about as expensive, if not a little more so, than a comparable quantity of carbohydrates. Is it cost-effective? That's hard to say. But as one researcher points out — if you can move a racehorse up six feet in a mile and a half, it doesn't really matter what it costs, does it?

# CHAPTER 6

## Vitamins

Vitamins: tiny organic compounds, with a huge impact on the health and well-being of your horse. Sometimes gleaned from the diet, sometimes manufactured within the digestive tract, vitamins have the power to promote and regulate virtually all of the body's normal functions, and they need be present only in minute amounts.

Researchers have classified vitamins into two categories which describe how the vitamins are absorbed, stored, and excreted by the body: fat-soluble, and water-soluble. Vitamins A, D, E, and K are fat-soluble vitamins, which tend to be stored in the body (and thus can build up toxicities if there is an excess), while the B vitamins and vitamin C are water-soluble, meaning that any excess not used quickly by the body tends to be excreted rather than stored.

Vitamins can also be classified according to their source. Under normal conditions, the horse quite efficiently produces his own vitamins C, D, and niacin (one of the B-complex vitamins) from other organic molecules he ingests, and the beneficial microbes living in his cecum and large intestine, as part of their symbiotic bargain, produce all of the other B vitamins as well as vitamin K. Only vitamins A and E are not produced within the horse's body, and must be obtained from vegetable matter in the diet.

There is still much we don't know about vitamins, and much that is misunderstood. One of the most common misconceptions about vitamins is that "if some is good, more is better." Horses can become vitamin-deficient, and these deficiencies can have devastating effects on his normal functions, but equally dangerous are toxicities from an overdose — a real possibility with some (but not all) of the vitamins. Further, different species have different vitamin requirements, so assumptions extrapolated from

> ## AT A GLANCE
>
> - Forage provides horses with an excellent daily dose of the vitamins they need.
>
> - Vitamin requirements vary little among horses.
>
> - Horses recovering from illness or infection might require vitamin supplements. So might poor eaters and horses exposed to high stress.
>
> - Vitamins are either fat-soluble or water-soluble.

human medicine might not necessarily apply to horses. Vitamin requirements don't really vary with the amount of work a horse does, either     the pleasure horse and high-performance athlete have almost identical needs. And while we frequently succumb to marketing ploys designed to convince us that our horses are in need of supplemental vitamins in their diet, the reality is that horses usually receive an excellent daily dose of the vitamins they require — those they cannot manufacture for themselves — from their forage (pasture or hay).

Vitamin excesses or deficiencies extreme enough actually to cause symptoms are pretty rare in horses. That's not to say however, that every diet provides absolutely optimum levels of vitamins. It's quite possible for a horse to be receiving enough vitamins for maintenance metabolism, but not for maximum beneficial health effects.

For example, a real vitamin E deficiency only occurs when a horse takes in less than 10 to 15 International Units (IU) per kilogram of his bodyweight in the dry diet. This is a level which is easily exceeded by most feeds. But studies have demonstrated that a higher level of vitamin E, along the lines of 50 to 100 IU/kg (more than is delivered by most feeds), might increase a horse's resistance to infections and to exertion-induced muscle damage. This is a case where some supplementation might produce a beneficial effect over and above what's required nutritionally. Biotin, which we'll discuss more in a minute, is another vitamin which is often fed in excess of the amounts a horse strictly requires to live, because it's reputed to have a beneficial effect on hoof growth and quality. But it's important to realize that in some cases, such effects might be more old horseman's lore than fact. Research is still ongoing, and each vitamin must be considered individually before you do any supplementing.

## SHOULD YOU SUPPLEMENT?

Vitamin supplementation might be beneficial in cases like the following:

• for horses on a high-grain, low-forage diet (such as youngsters in heavy race training), or for those on very poor-quality forage, or eating hay that is more than a year old. Vitamins tend to break down over time in stored feed. For example, there is a 9.5% loss of vitamin A activity in hay every month.

• for horses receiving prolonged antibiotic treatment for illness or infection. Broad-spectrum antibiotics inhibit the growth of the beneficial cecal and intestinal bacteria, which inhibits their production of B vitamins and vitamin K.

• for horses in high-stress situations, such as frequent traveling, showing, or racing.

• for horses who are eating poorly — for example, those recovering from surgery or illness.

• for horses who are anemic — although the source of the anemia should be determined and treated, first and foremost.

Vitamins in feed can decompose when exposed to sunlight, heat, air, or the processes that feed goes through in commercial packaging (such as grinding or cooking). Losses during long-term feed storage are greatest for vitamins A, D, K, and thiamin (B1). A is the most crucial of these since the horse does not manufacture this vitamin within his own system. Furthermore, some vitamins are incompatible with each other or with minerals that might also be in the feed. For example, most vitamins are prone to oxidative destruction by iron, copper, sulfates, sulfides, phosphates, and carbonates, all of which might be present in a feed or a vitamin/mineral supplement. The B vitamin thiamin (B1) is incompatible with riboflavin (B2), and both are incompatible with cobalamin (B12) in the presence of light. So feed manufacturers might go to great lengths to protect the vitamins' activity and efficacy, by coating them with gelatin, wax, sugar, or ethylcellulose — harmless, fortunately, to the horse in the amounts required. These compounds might make up a large part of the composition of a powdered or pelleted vitamin/mineral supplement. (Interestingly, it's very difficult to cover vitamins with any sort of protective coating in a liquid format, so many of the liquid supplements rich in B vitamins, iron, and copper, sold as "blood builders," might actually have very little active vitamin content.)

## VITAMIN PROFILES

Here's a primer on the function of each of the vitamins important to the horse, beginning with the fat-soluble vitamins.

### VITAMIN A

FUNCTION: Vitamin A, also called retinol, is important for the maintenance of good vision, particularly at night. It is also an important factor in bone and muscle growth of young horses, in reproduction, and in healthy skin.

SOURCES: Horses must satisfy all of their daily vitamin A requirement from their diets. Fortunately, green forages and yellow vegetables (such as carrots) are an excellent source of vitamin A's main precursor, beta-carotene, which is broken down by enzymes in the small intestine. The converted vitamin A is then stored in the liver, which can retain a three- to six-month supply, releasing it back into the bloodstream as the horse's body requires (or excreting it if there is an excess).

Not all of the carotenoid pigments the horse takes in on a daily basis are converted to vitamin A; some are absorbed intact and transported to body tissue such as the fat, skin, and ovaries for use and storage. (In the ovaries, beta-carotene has been shown to be involved in the control of progesterone secretion by the corpus luteum, making it a key player in the control of ovulation, embryo implantation, and the maintenance of pregnancy.) A deficiency of beta-carotene interferes with these functions, and interestingly, cannot be corrected by feeding more vitamin A, as the conversion doesn't seem to be wholly reversible.

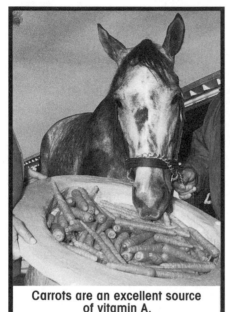

**Carrots are an excellent source of vitamin A.**

SIGNS OF DEFICIENCY: General signs of a vitamin A deficiency include a depressed appetite, weight loss, a dull haircoat, night blindness (distinguishable from periodic ophthalmia, or moon-blindness, by characteristically cloudy corneas), excessive tearing of the eyes, anemia, and even convulsive seizures. Long-term deficiencies might cause abortion in broodmares, and stallions might suffer decreased libido and soft, flabby testicles. Under normal conditions, the only way a horse can develop a vitamin A deficiency is if he is deprived of hay or pasture for more than six months (allowing time to deplete the stores in the liver). But if horses are going to be fed on very old hay or poor pasture for an extended period of time, vitamin A supplementation is a good idea.

Like all of the fat-soluble vitamins, vitamin A is poorly transported across the placenta. Thus, foals are born vitamin

A-deficient. Provided the mare's diet has sufficient beta-carotene, she will provide vitamin A to her foal in her colostrum, but if the foal's colostrum intake is insufficient, the deficiency will persist. Vitamin A-deficient foals might suffer from diarrhea, though they are not usually night-blind.

Signs of Toxicity: Horses can experience vitamin A toxicity, though as a rule it only occurs when an owner over-supplements the diet. In one study where foals were deliberately fed vitamin A in quantities exceeding 20,000 IU/kg, the results included stunted growth, scaly skin, increased bone size, bone fragility, and decreased blood clotting, leading to internal hemorrhages. There has been no demonstrated benefit to horses by feeding more than 2,000 to 3,000 IU/kg per day.

### VITAMIN D

SOURCES: Vitamin D is the "sunshine vitamin," created through chemical reactions of ultraviolet rays from the sun with 7-dehydrocholesterol (synthesized in the horse's skin) and ergosterol (in the dead leaves of plants). The chlorophyll in living plants blocks out ultraviolet rays, and it is only after plants have been cut and exposed to sunlight (as in sun-cured hay) that vitamin D begins to be present.

FUNCTION: Vitamin D assists in maintaining plasma calcium concentrations by interacting with parathyroid hormone (PTH) and calcitonin. This has the effect of increasing the absorption of both calcium and phosphorus from the intestine, with an indirect impact on bone mineralization.

SIGNS OF DEFICIENCY: A vitamin D deficiency results in rickets in the young of most species (including humans). The bones become soft and bendable, resulting in bowed legs and emaciation, and in severe cases, the affected animal will be reluctant to stand. But rickets *per se* have not been observed in horses with vitamin D deficiencies. Pony foals deprived of sunlight for five months did demonstrate decreased bone strength, and slower growth and feed intake, as well as irregular growth plates (visible on radiographs), however.

Most horses are unlikely to ever need vitamin D supplementation. Hay contains approximately 2,000 IU/kg of vitamin D when it is freshly baled, though like all vitamins, it degrades over time, at a rate of about 7.5% per month. Hay that is more than a year old might not, therefore, meet a horse's vitamin D needs, but as long as the horse receives a few hours of sunlight a day, this should be of no consequence. However, stabled horses which are not allowed access to direct sunlight for months on end should be provided in their diets with a level of 800 IU/kg (in the total diet) for growth, pregnancy, and lactation, or 300 IU/kg for normal maintenance.

SIGNS OF TOXICITY: The most common of all vitamin "overdoses," vitamin D toxicity occurs as a result of indiscriminate supplementation (either oral or injectable). Excess vitamin D is stored in the liver, and the effects are cumulative, becoming more obvious after a period of several weeks. They include calcium deposits which collect in the heart valves and walls, the walls of large blood vessels, and the kidney, diaphragm, salivary glands, and gastric mucosa. The result is decreased exercise tolerance, weight loss, stiffness, a decrease in spontaneous activity (with flexor tendons and suspensories often sensitive to palpation), an increased resting heartrate, the development of heart murmurs, and increased water intake and urination. Toxicosis can be confirmed by elevated plasma concentrations.

### VITAMIN E

FUNCTION: Versatile vitamin E enhances immune function, is essential for cellular respiration, is involved in DNA synthesis, and improves the absorption and storage of vitamin A, among other effects. But most importantly, vitamin E and the mineral selenium are partners in protecting the horse's body tissues — especially cell membranes, enzymes, and other intracellular compounds — from the damaging effects of oxidation. Inadequate amounts of either one in the horse's system assure that there will be considerable free-radical damage to the tissues.

SOURCES: Vitamin E is the only vitamin other than A which horses must source from their diets. Green growing forage contains good amounts of vitamin E, but from 30 to 80% of the vitamin's activity is lost during the process of cutting and baling hay, and nearly all of the vitamin E is destroyed in high-moisture feeds such as haylage. Because not all horses are lucky enough to have good pasture year-round, commercial grain rations are usually fortified with stable forms of vitamin E.

SIGNS OF DEFICIENCY: Usually grouped with selenium deficiency, which we'll discuss in the next chapter, vitamin E deficiency can cause muscle wastage and malformation (sometimes called "white muscle disease" in foals), subcutaneous edema, infertility, a stiff, stilted "base-wide" gait, a swollen tongue, and inflammation of fatty tissues, or steatitis, by insoluble pigments (often called "yellow-fat disease"), especially in foals. A mild deficiency of vitamin E might only produce a decrease in the horse's immune response, and in foals, a slower growth rate.

SIGNS OF TOXICITY: Horses can easily suffer from selenium excesses (selenium has the lowest toxicity level of any mineral important to the equine diet), but vitamin E is relatively non-toxic. Because of this, some feed manufacturers use it as a natural anti-oxidant in their grain rations to help prevent spoilage, leading to feed tag values that are far higher than the nutritional requirement of most horses.

No clinical signs of vitamin E toxicosis have been produced, but because very high levels can interfere with the absorption of other fat-soluble vitamins, a conservative maximum level of 1,000 IU/kg in the diet is generally recommended.

### VITAMIN K

FUNCTION: Vitamin K is primarily an activator for blood clotting factors, though it also participates in the activation of other proteins throughout the body.

SOURCES: There are several forms of vitamin K that occur in nature, some in green leafy plants, and others manufactured by the horse's cecal bacteria. While the natural forms of vitamin K are fat-soluble, they are converted to a water-soluble format before they are stored in the horse's liver. As a result, vitamin K is easily excreted in the urine and so the body does not tend to retain a large supply. However, the combination of vitamin K ingested in pasture or hay and that produced in the cecum is considered adequate for any horse's needs under almost all circumstances.

One exception is a vitamin K deficiency induced by sweet clover poisoning. An anticoagulant called dicoumarol (chemically related to warfarin) sometimes occurs in moldy sweet clover hay or haylage. If the moldy hay is ingested over a period of several weeks, the horse's synthesis of vitamin K-dependent clotting factors is impaired. The problem occurs most often in cattle, but has been reported in both horses and sheep. If untreated, mortality and the risk of abortion in broodmares can be high.

Vitamin K deficiencies also can result from anything that compromises the gut flora — such as severe colic or diarrhea, abdominal surgery, or antibacterial drugs. Chronic liver disease also can be a factor. And because newborn foals are deficient at birth, vitamin K injections often are recommended to prevent hemorrhagic diseases.

SIGNS OF DEFICIENCY: A long-term vitamin K deficiency decreases blood coagulation. Bleeding from the nose is frequently one of the first signs in horses. Hematomas and/or internal bleeding might also occur, and if sufficient blood is lost, the horse will have pale mucous membranes, a rapid and irregular heartbeat, and be depressed and weak.

SIGNS OF TOXICITY: Vitamin K toxicity is rare, though injections of the water-soluble form can be dangerous, causing acute renal failure and death. Oral forms of the vitamin appear to be innocuous, fortunately. No ideal levels of vitamin

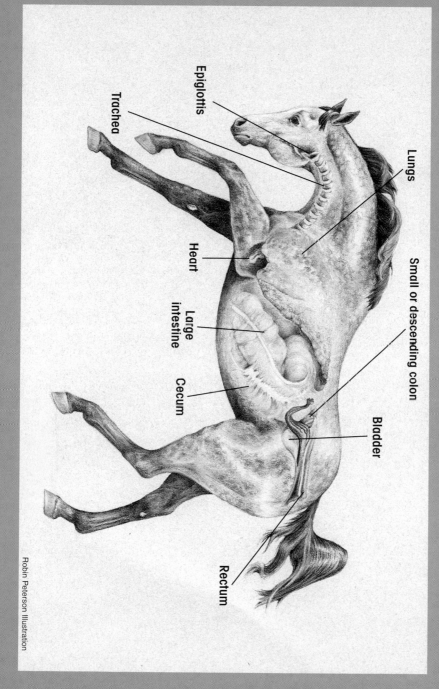

Viscera of the Horse

Epiglottis

Trachea

Lungs

Heart

Small or descending colon

Large intestine

Cecum

Bladder

Rectum

Robin Peterson Illustration

65

The horse in the photo above is in poor condition as evidenced
by coat condition and prominence of ribs and hips;
the horse below is lean but racing fit.

The horse in the photo above is in excellent condition and carrying an appropriate amount of weight for his size; the horse below is overweight — notice the thickness of the neck and fat deposits on the hindquarters.

By late fall, the nutrient value of this pasture has dropped considerably; below, hay cut past mid-bloom is stemmy and contains a number of sud-heads, an indication that the nutritive value of the hay is past its best.

In winter, horses which live outside need forage and hay provides that requirement; below, weanlings get valuable nutrients from pasture grass and hay.

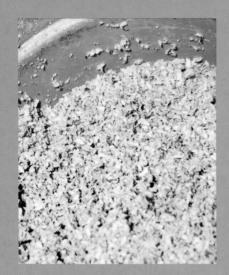 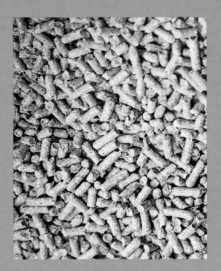

Clockwise from top left: beet pulp, "complete feed,"
extruded feed, and barley.

A well-organized feed room (above);
below, sweet feed, a staple in many barns.

Horses not only love apples and treats such as carrots, but they get important nutrients from these sources.

K have been established for the horse, but in a case where supplementation is called for (for example, after a course of antibiotics, or after a serious colic), the usual recommendation is for three to five mg/kg of body weight/day, mixed into the feed, for a week or more.

## WATER-SOLUBLE VITAMINS

### THIAMIN (VITAMIN B1)

FUNCTION: Thiamin plays an important role in carbohydrate metabolism and in nerve transmission and stimulation.

SOURCES: While horses do receive good concentrations of thiamin from their intestinal bacteria, several studies have determined that they also require some more from their diets. Fortunately, most green forage is an excellent source of thiamin (and indeed, all of the "B-complex" vitamins), as is brewer's yeast.

SIGNS OF DEFICIENCY: Thiamin deficiency can occur when horses eat bracken ferns (which contain a compound that inhibits its absorption), but is otherwise uncommon. In studies where the deficiency has been artificially produced, horses showed signs of anorexia, loss of coordination, skipped heartbeats, and unusually cold hooves, ears, and muzzles.

SIGNS OF TOXICITY: Thiamin toxicity is very unlikely. Dietary intakes of up to 1,000 times the recommended amount have been safely administered to horses without any ill effects. However, if doses of 1,000 to 2,000 mg of thiamin are injected, it might produce a slowed pulse rate and a mild tranquilizing effect (a result which has been disputed in some research). Certainly thiamin has the reputation, in some circles, of being a tranquilizer, but it is important to keep in mind that large doses of this vitamin have produced convulsions, labored breathing, and death by respiratory paralysis in dogs, mice, and rabbits. High doses of thiamin also have been suspected, on occasion, to cause the opposite effect in horses — over-excitation.

### RIBOFLAVIN (VITAMIN B2)

FUNCTION: Oxidative energy metabolism depends on riboflavin, and deficiencies (which have not been documented naturally, but have been induced in experimental situations) compromise the tissues most in need of oxygen during strenuous exercise.

SOURCES: Fresh forage and yeast supplements are two good sources of riboflavin, a vitamin also synthesized by the gut flora.

SIGNS OF DEFICIENCY: Signs of riboflavin deficiency include decreased feed intake, scaly skin and a dull haircoat, inflammation of the lips and tongue, colon ulcers, diarrhea, anestrus (lack of heat periods in the mare), and a rear-end muscular weakness. Irritation to the eyes also results, with increased tearing, sensitivity to light, and inflammation of the surrounding tissues. Some years ago riboflavin was thought to be involved with periodic ophthalmia (moon-blindness); more recent research, however, has absolved it of this responsibility, pointing the finger instead at infection by the parasite *onchocerca cervicalis*, or an aggravated immune response.

SIGNS OF TOXICITY: Horses tolerate high levels of riboflavin very well, and no signs of toxicity have been documented.

### NIACIN (NICOTINIC ACID) AND PANTOTHENIC ACID

FUNCTION: Niacin is considered a B vitamin but has no numerical designation. It does share qualities of the other B vitamins, however, being important in the regulation of energy metabolism, especially the processing of carbohydrates, amino acids, and fats. Another B vitamin, pantothenic acid (formerly designated vitamin B3), also is involved in the metabolism of carbohydrates, fats, and proteins.

SOURCES: Both pantothenic acid and niacin are widely available in virtually all vegetable matter.

SIGNS OF DEFICIENCY AND TOXICITY: Actual niacin or pantothenic acid deficiency — or excess, for that matter — has not been described in horses. Theoretically, because like the other members of the B family, these two vitamins are involved in biochemical reactions in the body, the symptoms of deficiency (if clinically induced) would tend to resemble those described for the other B vitamins.

### PYROXIDINE (VITAMIN B6)

FUNCTION: Amino acid metabolism is the main function for pyroxidine, but this vitamin also is involved in glycogen utilization, in the synthesis of epinephrine (adrenaline) and norepinephrine, and in the metabolism of fats.

SIGNS OF DEFICIENCY AND TOXICITY: Again, no signs of deficiency or excess have actually been documented in the horse because pyroxidine is widely available in the diet and is also manufactured by the intestinal flora, though in humans, high doses of pyroxidine administered on a daily basis have produced signs of sensory nervous system dysfunctions. Dietary levels of up to 50 times the nutritional requirement are considered safe for horses

### BIOTIN

FUNCTION: Most horsepeople are familiar with biotin as a supplement for hooves, but fewer know that it is considered one of the B-complex vitamins. Its primary role is as a coenzyme in several crucial, but complex, chemical reactions related to metabolism, including the synthesis of glycerol for body fats, RNA, and DNA.

SOURCES: Biotin is readily available in plant material, and manufactured, to a certain level, by the gut microflora. However, researchers debate whether the amount a horse's system produces is adequate for his daily needs. Biotin deficiencies in fish, mink, foxes, pigs, and turkeys have been reported, and, intriguingly, the symptoms that result often include skin, footpad, and/or periople lesions that provide a ready comparison to the thin, shelly hooves some horses grow.

Biotin is a vitamin with which a distinction might be made

between the horse's need for it on a nutritional level and the good it might be able to do when administered in much larger amounts. Feeding higher concentrations of biotin makes it, in essence, a pharmaceutical, which has been shown in some cases to improve the quality and speed of hoof horn growth.

Unfortunately, no one has yet established an absolutely optimal level of biotin. The amounts included in most of the popular hoof supplements (from 10 to 30 mg or more) are well above what is considered the base requirement. Fortunately, high levels of biotin are well-tolerated, making biotin supplementation a relatively harmless therapy, even if its results vary from horse to horse and might take six to nine months to become obvious.

### COBALAMIN (VITAMIN $B_{12}$) AND FOLACIN

FUNCTION: Both of these vitamins are needed for the synthesis of red blood cells, and a deficiency of either will result in anemia. In addition to this role, $B_{12}$ also is required for the production of propionate, a major energy source derived from the fermentation of carbohydrates.

SOURCES: While folacin can be found in green forage, $B_{12}$ is unique among vitamins in that it is synthesized in nature only by micro-organisms. Although the gut flora seem to produce ample $B_{12}$, the vitamin is often administered to high-performance horses to enhance performance, treat or prevent anemia, and stimulate the appetite. So far, there is no evidence to support the belief that supplemental $B_{12}$ does any of these things, though severely anemic or heavily parasitized horses do appear to respond to it. (It should be pointed out that it is likely far more valuable to treat this type of horse through deworming and a proper diet than through $B_{12}$ injections, which only increase plasma concentrations of the vitamin for a short period of time.)

SIGNS OF DEFICIENCY/TOXICITY: Neither has been reported in horses to date.

### VITAMIN C (ASCORBIC ACID)

FUNCTION: Most of us are familiar with vitamin C but have heard very little of its function or requirement by horses. It is an anti-oxidant, which protects fats, proteins, and membranes from free radicals. In addition, it enhances the formation of bone and teeth, aids in the utilization of several of the B vitamins as well as cholesterol and glucose, and improves the intestinal absorption of iron. On top of this, it's a component of the connective tissue collagen and several amino acids.

SOURCES: Humans are one of the few species which, because of the lack of a crucial enzyme, do not synthesize their own vitamin C from glucose in their livers. For most species, including the horse, vitamin C does not need to be taken in daily from the diet, and in fact there is no demonstrated dietary requirement of this vitamin for horses — just as well, since most equines aren't big on citrus fruits.

SIGNS OF DEFICIENCY: The effects of a vitamin C deficiency do not occur in horses, though it is suspected that horses over the age of 20 years, or those who have been ill or stressed, might sometimes suffer low plasma concentrations of ascorbic acid which could be associated with wound infections, bleeding from the nose, and an increased susceptibility to disease. Some cases of infertility in both mares and stallions also have been reported to improve with the supplementation of vitamin C, but this has yet to be confirmed by research. In any case, oral vitamin C has been shown to be poorly absorbed by the horse, and intramuscular injections of the vitamin tend to cause marked tissue irritation. Intravenous administration has been tried, but the body so efficiently eliminates this water-soluble compound that plasma concentrations only remained elevated for a few hours. The form that is sometimes included in feeds, on the off chance it might have some beneficial effect, is ascorbylpalmitate, which horses (but few other species) can absorb fairly well.

Next chapter, we'll explore the vitamins' "partners in crime": minerals.

# CHAPTER 7

## *Minerals*

**O**f all the ingredients of a horse's diet, minerals are unique. They make up only the tiniest fraction of the weight of the daily ration, yet they're critically important for literally dozens of daily bodily functions. They contribute no energy and contain no carbon. In fact, essentially, they're rocks — and it can be difficult to imagine their being digested by a horse (or a human, for that matter).

But without their participation, horses could not metabolize fats, proteins, or carbohydrates; their muscles and nerves would not function normally; and their bones could not support their own weight. Minerals help the blood transport oxygen throughout the body, maintain the body's acid/base and fluid balances, and are necessary components of virtually every enzyme the horse needs for everyday metabolism. They are integral parts of some vitamins, hormones, and amino acids. Yet they make up only about 4% of the horse's total body weight (as compared to 30% to 35% fats, carbohydrates, and proteins, and about 60% water). In the case of minerals, a little bit means a lot.

Minerals are generally divided into two categories: macrominerals, which are needed in larger quantities (relatively speaking) in the daily diet, and microminerals, or trace minerals, which are needed only in infinitesimal amounts (usually expressed as parts per million, or ppm — or sometimes as the equivalent unit, mg/kg). Macrominerals, which include calcium, phosphorus, magnesium, sodium, potassium, sulfur, and chlorine (as chloride), are described in parts per hundred, or percentages. To provide some perspective, the micromineral "unit," ppm, is 10,000 times smaller. Iodine, manganese, iron, cobalt, zinc, copper, and selenium are all considered trace minerals necessary to the horse — though the optimum amounts required are, in some cases, still in dispute.

> ## AT A GLANCE
>
> • Minerals help the equine body perform dozens of daily functions.
>
> • Minerals help metabolize fats, carbohydrates, and proteins.
>
> • Minerals fall into two general categories: macrominerals, which are needed in relatively large quantities, and include calcium, and microminerals such as iodine.

The roles of various minerals in the functioning of the equine body are not always clear-cut. There are some trace minerals which seem to play a role in metabolism, but have not yet been proven to produce any symptoms of deficiency when they are not present: these "mystery minerals" include vanadium, tin, silicon, nickel, chromium, molybdenum, fluorine, and arsenic. It's interesting to note that some of these are also minerals which can be categorized as "heavy metals." They are capable of doing significant damage if ingested in large enough amounts. Potentially toxic are lead, arsenic, nickel, aluminum, and cadmium, all heavy metals which might have a tiny role to play in nutrition. Ongoing research will likely reveal more about these ingredients in time.

All minerals can have an adverse effect if present in the diet in large enough amounts, but in most cases there is a broad safety zone. Within that safe range, feeding the minimum amount of a mineral might be just as effective as feeding the maximum amount — and often, considerably less expensive. Of course, the companies who market feed supplements might prefer that you believe otherwise!

Making matters even more complicated is the fact that some minerals have "relationships": the amount of one mineral present might affect the absorption and utilization of another. Calcium and phosphorus are the most famous partners. They are both essential to the growth and repair of healthy bone, but must be present in a certain proportion (with at least as much calcium as phosphorus, never the reverse) in order to do their job. Copper, zinc, and iron (with the possible addition of magnesium and manganese) form another linkage, which has received a good deal of scrutiny by researchers exploring developmental bone abnormalities in young horses. And there might be many more connections we don't yet fully understand.

Finally, the absorption of minerals in the horse's gut varies widely. Most of these elements can bind in a number of different molecules, some of which are easier for the horse's digestive system to break down than others. (Zinc, for example, can be found in the diet as zinc carbonate, zinc sulfate, or zinc oxide, to name only three.) The result is that, of the amount of a mineral listed on a product's feed tag, only a very small percentage might actually be used by the horse. For example, the average absorption of calcium varies between 10% and 40%, while phosphorus is somewhat better utilized, at about 70%. Iron absorption ranges from 2% to 20%, with about 4% being the average. Zinc's range is from 5% all the way up to 90%, and between 25% and 75% of ingested magnesium is absorbed, with an average of 43%.

Feed company chemists have tried to address the absorption problem in a number of innovative ways, some more successful than others. Organic (plant) sources of minerals often are absorbed better than are the inorganic (artificial) sources feed companies might use to supplement a feed — but even this is not a hard-and-fast rule. For some minerals, absorption can be significantly improved by "chelating" them — a process which bonds minerals to two or more amino acids to form stable biochemical ring compounds, which can be metabolized as much as 300% to 500% more efficiently than their inorganic counterparts. Alas, there is no one magic formula for improving absorption, as what works for one mineral might be a dismal failure with another. This is true even with chelation, which produces very good results with some minerals (including most of the macrominerals) but not all.

Mineral absorption (roughly determined by measuring the amount of the mineral remaining in the manure, compared with the amount contained in the ingested feed) can also be affected by a whole host of other factors. The amount of other nutrients in the diet, such as fats, indigestible fiber, and vitamins, can all have an influence on mineral utilization; so can the pH balance of the gut (which affects the solubility of the minerals).

Nor is the mineral content of feeds etched in stone. It can vary with soil mineral concentrations, plant species, stage of maturity, and conditions at harvesting. All of these factors keep feed industry chemists on their toes as they formulate feeds and supplements for the horse's maximum benefit.

Still, there is much we *do* understand about the macrominerals, and at least some of the trace minerals. Here, then, is a rundown of the most important minerals in your horse's diet.

## CALCIUM AND PHOSPHORUS

FUNCTION: First on the feed tag, and in most discussions of minerals, is calcium, a versatile player best known for its role in bone structure and repair. Calcium makes up about 35% of the horse's bone structure, but it is also involved in a host of other functions, including cardiac muscle contraction, cell membrane integrity, glandular secretion, temperature regulation, and blood clotting mechanisms. The absorption efficiency of calcium seems to decline with age, and to range from as high as 70% in young horses to 50% or less in older ones.

It is almost impossible to discuss calcium without considering its partner, phosphorus, which is also essential to the growth and maintenance of healthy bones and teeth, as well as to energy metabolism and numerous cellular functions. It also plays an important role in late pregnancy and lactation, during which times a mare's phosphorus needs increase.

The ratio of calcium to phosphorus in the equine diet is crucial. Symptoms of deficiency will result if the horse does not receive at least as much calcium as phosphorus. That 1:1 ratio serves as a baseline, though interestingly, horses can tolerate quite a lot of calcium (more than five times the recommended level) provided the base level of phosphorus is adequate. Most researchers feel the ideal balance is about 1.2 parts calcium to 1 part phosphorus, up to about 1.6:1. Excess dietary phosphorus, in any form, binds calcium and prevents its absorption, but the same is not true in reverse; excess calcium has almost no effect on the absorption of phosphorus.

SIGNS OF DEFICIENCY AND TOXICITY: Symptoms of calcium deficiency (or excess phosphorus) can include developmental bone abnormalities in foals, "big head disease" (also called bran disease) in adult horses, decreased bone density, stiffness and possible lameness, weight loss, loose teeth, and fragile bones which fracture easily. Most of the same symptoms will occur if a phosphorus deficiency exists. Deficiencies of either mineral result in mobilization of these minerals from the bone — that is, they are drawn from the bone matrix and re-introduced to the blood plasma. In this way, while the bone is weakened, the other body functions to which calcium and phosphorus are pivotal are maintained.

Under most circumstances, horses eating forage have a hard time developing a calcium deficiency, as hay (especially legume hay) is calcium-rich. However, a diet very low in forage and high in grains (which are naturally high in phosphorus) can produce these symptoms. Historically, horses fed diets rich in wheat bran often developed this imbalance; today, it's rare. One of the few other causes of calcium deficiency in horses is the ingestion of plants containing high amounts of oxalate compounds, which inhibit calcium absorption. Plants like sorrel, dock, rhubarb, purslane, kikuyu grass, and lambsquarter can contain potentially harmful amounts of oxalates. They are primarily a problem for young horses, and might also cause diarrhea and gastroenteritis.

## SODIUM AND CHLORIDE

Even those for whom chemistry was never a strong subject know that sodium and chloride together make table salt. And the vast majority of horsemen know that salt is a crucial part of the equine diet.

FUNCTION: The two elements (Na+ and Cl-) are responsible for the regulation of all the horse's body fluids, as well as the conduction of electrical impulses in nerves and muscles, and are the most important of the minerals known as electrolytes (minerals which are lost in the sweat and urine during exercise stress). Chloride is also an essential ingredient of bile and is important in the formation of hydrochloric acid, a component of the gastric secretions necessary for digestion.

For maintenance, the horse's diet (as dry matter) should contain at least 0.25% salt (a level which will supply a maintenance level of 0.1% sodium), and if the horse is exercising hard enough to sweat on a regular basis, he should receive 0.75% salt per day. Exact chloride requirements for horses have not been established, but they are thought to be satisfied when the horse ingests enough salt to take care of his sodium requirements. (Salt is not a 50/50 proposition, by the way — chemistry being the complicated thing it is, salt works out to be about 39% sodium and 61% chloride.)

SOURCES: Many feeds contain less than 0.1% sodium, which is less than is needed even by horses who are idle. For this reason, horses should always have access to free-choice salt, in the form of a lick or in loose form. Alternatively, you can add additional salt to your horse's feed, though this is a less perfect solution — horses have a certain amount of "nutritional wisdom" when it comes to salt, and are best left to ingest the amount their bodies tell them they need. (Contrary to popular belief, this nutritional wisdom does not extend to other minerals — horses don't wake up with a craving for cobalt or manganese any more than we do.)

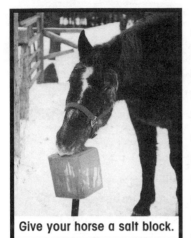

**Give your horse a salt block.**

When you provide salt to your horse, you can choose between salt blocks which are iodized, those with added trace minerals, and those which are just plain salt. While the trace mineral blocks are a good idea, they still contain mostly salt (about 95% on average), so should not be depended on to supply all of your horse's other mineral needs. Furthermore, some horses object to the taste of a trace-mineral block and thus will not ingest all the salt they require. The best solution might be to provide both plain or iodized salt, and a trace-mineral-plus-salt block, in your horse's pasture or stall, and give him the choice.

SIGNS OF DEFICIENCY: Because horses will usually consume salt in excess of their nutritional needs if it is available, salt deficiencies are almost as rare as real toxicities. However, such losses might occur in stressful situations, such as 100-mile endurance races in very hot, humid conditions. If a sodium chloride deficiency occurs rapidly, muscle contraction and chewing might become uncoordinated, sweating will decrease (with a corresponding decrease in performance), the gait might become unsteady, and plasma concentrations of both sodium and chloride will decrease while potassium will increase. Generally, however, a salt deficiency occurs more slowly and might only be noticeable because the horse begins to lick objects and surfaces which might have salt on them. If salt is not provided, he might become dehydrated and constipated, lose his appetite, and become weakened.

SIGNS OF TOXICITY: The absorption levels of sodium and chloride are quite high — from 75% to 95%, by most researchers' estimations. Excesses are readily excreted in the urine, provided the horse has access to fresh, clean water. The only time high salt intake (from adding too much salt to the feed, from drinking brine or sea-water out of desperation, or from a salt-block-munching habit) is likely to become a problem occurs when fresh water is restricted. Clinical signs of salt toxicity include colic, diarrhea, frequent urination, paralysis of the hind limbs, staggering and weakness, and eventually, death. It is treated by offering water in small amounts at frequent intervals; too much, too soon might produce cellular swelling and intracranial pressure problems, which can be very dangerous.

## POTASSIUM

FUNCTION: Potassium, designated by the chemical symbol K, is a crucial element of cellular osmotic pressure and the maintenance of the body's acid/base balance. It is also considered an electrolyte, and is usually the other major mineral horsemen are concerned about replacing when a horse is working hard.

SOURCES: Most forages contain between 1% and 4% potassium, plenty to satisfy the horse's daily requirement of about 0.4% — or even the hard-working horse's requirement of 0.6%. (Even most cereal grains, containing between 0.3% and 0.5% potassium, can usually fulfill the daily requirement without difficulty.)

Those who wish to increase their horse's potassium intake (usually in anticipation of, or in response to, high-stress competition) can do so with a commercial electrolyte product, or by adding 50 to 100 grams of "lite" or "low sodium" salt (half sodium chloride, and half potassium chloride — containing about 26% potassium) to the feed. Lite salt is available in most major supermarkets.

SIGNS OF DEFICIENCY: Without sufficient potassium, horses are prone to fatigue, muscle weakness, exercise intolerance, and decreased water and feed intake. Increased restlessness and spookiness, especially in response to loud noises, have also been reported. Because sweating increases potassium loss, both in the sweat itself and in the urine, deficiencies are a concern particularly for high-level three-day-event and endurance horses, particularly when they are training or competing in hot, humid conditions. Potential potassium losses also can be aggravated by the administration of diuretics such as Lasix (often used to treat racehorses with pulmonary hemorrhages, sometimes called "bleeders"), and are a risk in horses with diarrheal diseases such as Potomac Horse Fever. Outside of these conditions, however, potassium deficiencies are rare.

SIGNS OF TOXICITY: Excess potassium intake is not harmful, as it is readily excreted in the urine. The exception is horses which suffer from the genetic abnormality HYPP (hyperkalemic periodic paralysis), in which excess potassium tends to build up in the system. The disease, limited to Quarter Horses, Paints, and Appaloosas descended from the Impressive line, is treated nutritionally by keeping the dietary intake of potassium under 1% (usually by feeding a high-grain, low-forage diet, and avoiding particularly young forage and molasses, which also contains high amounts of the mineral). There are now grain rations with low potassium levels marketed specifically for HYPP horses.

## MAGNESIUM

FUNCTION: About 60% of the body's store of magnesium is tied up in the skeletal structure, but it is also an important activator of many enzymes.

SOURCES: The horse's magnesium needs of about 0.1% per day are easily met by a normal diet (the magnesium content of most horse feeds is between 0.1% and 0.3%). Magnesium absorption tends to be in the 40% range, with utilization of added dietary sources, such as magnesium oxide or magnesium sulfate, sometimes somewhat better (up to about 70%).

SIGNS OF DEFICIENCY AND TOXICITY: Neither magnesium deficiencies nor toxicities have been reported in horses being fed normal diets, except in the rare case of lactating mares which have demonstrated tetany (intermittent muscle spasms, similar to those produced by the disease tetanus) as a possible result of a high-potassium, low-magnesium diet and high levels of magnesium being excreted in the milk. The condition is far more common in milking cattle, which do not absorb magnesium as efficiently as horses.

Experimentally induced magnesium deficiencies in foals have produced muscle tremors, nervousness, uncoordinated movement, and eventually, collapse, convulsive paddling, and death. There was also, on autopsy, some mineralization (deposits of calcium and phosphorus) in the aorta. There have been no studies on the effects of high-magnesium diets, though horses apparently have a high tolerance for this mineral.

## SULFUR

FUNCTION: We don't tend to think of sulfur as an important mineral, but it is an essential constituent of several amino acids (methionine, cystine, and cystcine) as well as the B vitamins biotin and thiamin, and a number of other important molecules such as insulin, taurine, and chondroitin sulfate, a component of cartilage, bone, tendons, and blood vessels. The concentration of sulfur in the body is highest in hooves and hair, which both contain the protein keratin (4% sulfur). Overall, sulfur makes up about 0.15% of the horse's total body weight.

SOURCES: Despite its importance, the exact sulfur requirements of the horse have not yet been determined. Most horse feeds contain about 0.15% organic sulfur, which seems to be enough to meet daily requirements. Inorganic sulfur is not readily absorbed by the horse, but organic (bound into amino acids) is.

SIGNS OF DEFICIENCY AND TOXICITY: Sulfur deficiencies have not been reported in horses, though in other species it produces decreased appetite, growth and milk production. In pigs and ruminants, excess dietary sulfur interferes with copper absorption, but so far there is no evidence that this occurs in horses. In fact, no side-effects have been noted from high sulfur intake in equines, as the mineral is easily excreted in the urine and feces.

## TRACE MINERALS

### *SELENIUM*

FUNCTION: Although it is needed in infinitesimal amounts, selenium is a mineral which has received a lot of press in recent years. Selenium and vitamin E function in a partnership which helps protect body tissues from free-radical damage which occurs during oxidation (the conversion of foodstuffs into energy). In particular, they act as a defense mechanism against damage to cell membranes and enzymes. While vitamin E blocks free radical attacks on lipids, selenium is a component of the enzyme glutathione peroxidase, which helps prevent the formation of free radicals and destroys lipid peroxidases which are released into the cells. This dynamic duo works best when both are present in the correct amounts.

SIGNS OF TOXICITY: Selenium is a tricky mineral, for several reasons. First, unlike most minerals which have a broad safety range, selenium has a very low threshold of toxicity for horses — only a few parts per million beyond the recommended levels. (Most other livestock species have a much higher tolerance, partly because their absorption rates are lower than horses'.) Thus the assumption that "if some is good, more is better" is a particularly dangerous one for this mineral — and the effects of selenium toxicity can be worse than the effects of a deficiency. They can include patchy sweating, blind staggers, colic, diarrhea, and increased heart and respiration rates if acute (as in, for example, when a horse is given selenium injections), or when chronic, loss of hair, especially in the mane and tail, the cracking of hooves around the coronary band, and occasionally hooves that, shockingly, slough off completely.

The selenium content of various feeds varies depending on where the plants were grown — and across North America, the soil content of selenium fluctuates significantly. Some areas are so selenium-deficient that crops grown there are considered to contain no selenium at all, necessitating supplementation. Some locations have adequate selenium in the soil, and others actually have toxic concentrations of selenium, making any supplementation positively reckless. Pockets where toxic levels exist are located in California, Colorado, Idaho, Montana, Oregon, South Dakota, Utah, and Wyoming; however, all of these states except Wyoming also report areas that are deficient. The Great Lakes region, and almost all of Canada except for southern Manitoba, Saskatchewan, and Alberta, tend to be severely selenium-deficient.

This extreme variation from region to region is the reason that regulations exist, in Canada and in most of the United States, to make sure feed companies print a warning to consumers if there is selenium added to a feed. What might be appropriate to feed in one region would be a very poor choice in another.

Because the toxicity threshold of selenium is so low (between two and five ppm), you should be aware of the selenium content of your local soils (and thus, your pasture and your hay) before you choose a vitamin-E-and-selenium supplement, or a selenium-added feed, for your horse. Even some trace-mineral salt blocks contain added selenium, so be sure to check the label before you place it in the pasture. Information on the selenium content of your local soils can be obtained from your local agriculture extension specialist, or even your local feed store or co-op.

SIGNS OF DEFICIENCY: The level of selenium currently recommended for horses is between 0.1 ppm and 0.3 ppm (dry matter), though some researchers feel that this is a little conservative. In mild deficiencies, the only symptom might be an increased susceptibility to disease, due to a depressed immune system, and/or decreased fertility in breeding stock.

Far less common are severe selenium deficiencies, which are characterized by weakness, impaired movement, difficulty in swallowing, impaired cardiac function, and respiratory distress. Selenium deficiencies have also been implicated in certain types of "tying up" in performance horses. Young foals, from birth to about four weeks of age, are most likely to demonstrate clinical symptoms (which occur as a result of inadequate selenium intake by the dam during pregnancy). They might develop muscle pain, an inability to nurse, and a stilted hopping gait in the rear legs, or be stillborn or die within a few days of birth. In areas where selenium deficiency is a documented problem in foals, the dam should receive supplementation throughout her pregnancy, and the foal given a vitamin-E-and-selenium injection just after birth.

### IODINE

FUNCTION: Iodine is a specialist. It is essential for the synthesis of thyroid hormones thyroxin (T4) and tri-iodothyronine (T3), which help regulate basal metabolism — and unlike some other minerals, which fulfill numerous functions, this is iodine's only known role in the diet.

The horse's estimated daily requirement of iodine is 0.1 ppm (or 1-2 mg per 500 kg horse per day), and like selenium (and unlike practically every other mineral), iodine's toxicity threshold is quite low, about 5 ppm (40 mg/horse/day).

SOURCES: Most horse feeds contain between 0.05 and 0.2 ppm (dry matter) of iodine, but some might contain as much as 2 ppm, depending on the soils in which the feed was grown. Thus, it is possible for horses to become iodine-deficient on a normal diet, though feeding an iodized or trace-mineral salt (at a level of as little as half an ounce a day) can easily prevent deficiencies. It is also possible for horses to ingest toxic amounts of iodine, either as a result of over-supplementing with iodized salt (if it is more than 4% of the total diet), or by feeding seaweed (kelp) or supplements containing it, on top of a feed already enriched with iodine.

Seaweed might contain as much as 1,850 ppm of iodine — and at that level, as little as 0.7 oz. a day might be harmful. Pregnant and lactating mares seem to be less tolerant of high levels of iodine than other horses. Overall, in recent years, reports of iodine toxicosis have been more frequent than reports of deficiencies. Some researchers have chalked this up to overzealous supplementing by well-meaning owners.

SIGNS OF DEFICIENCY AND TOXICITY: Both iodine deficiencies and excesses produce very similar symptoms — they both result in a goiter, a swelling of the thyroid gland on the underside of the horse's throat, just under the jaw. This can make it rather difficult to discern, at first glance, whether you are dealing with too much iodine or too little. The best way to determine which is the problem is to evaluate the iodine levels in the diet, as blood plasma levels of thyroid hormones can fluctuate quite a lot. If no seaweed or supplemental sources of iodine are being fed, then chances are you are dealing with a deficiency.

Other symptoms of an iodine imbalance are a dry, lusterless haircoat, hair loss, decreased growth and decreased bone calcification in young horses, lethargy and drowsiness, and cold intolerance and possible hypothermia (low body temperature). Sometimes an iodine deficiency (but not an excess) will produce a thickened skin due to the accumulation of mucinous material under the skin of the limbs. This is called myxedema.

As with many mineral imbalances, detrimental effects of too much or too little iodine are most obvious in foals. Severely affected foals (usually born to mares with iodine imbalances) are weak, have difficulty standing, suffer persistent hypothermia (with an abnormally low rectal temperature of less than 100 degrees Celsius), and have a weak sucking response. They might suffer respiratory distress, as well, and have noticeably enlarged thyroids. Most die within a few days of birth. Those who survive might suffer from various bone and joint abnormalities. Iodine toxicosis, but not deficiency, might also increase a horse's susceptibility to infectious diseases.

## COPPER

FUNCTION: This mineral is a component of several enzymes involved in the synthesis and maintenance of elastic connective tissue, the mobilization of iron stores (more on iron in a moment), and synthesis of the body pigment melanin, as well as being involved in bone collagen stabilization.

The liver regulates copper metabolism by storing it or excreting it in the bile. Its absorption in the gut might be influenced by the levels of other minerals, such as zinc, iron, and molybdenum, making it somewhat difficult to estimate how much dietary copper is utilized; but because copper toxicity only occurs at relatively high levels in horses (in contrast to some other species — sheep in particular are very sensitive to it), most feed companies err on the side of generosity when it comes to copper, in the hopes that enough will be absorbed to meet the horse's needs. The exact optimum levels of copper in the equine diet have not yet been established. The National Research Council recommends a level of 10 ppm, which many researchers feel is low. (Some have suggested a level of 50 ppm for creep-feeding foals, and at least 25 ppm for weanlings up to 12 months of age.)

SIGNS OF DEFICIENCY: Copper deficiencies might play a role in developmental orthopedic diseases of young horses (though some researchers now believe its participation might have been over-rated), and the deficiencies also have been implicated in ruptures of the aorta or uterine arteries in aged foaling mares.

Real copper deficiencies have rarely been noted in horses. A foal gettibg inadequate amounts of copper might have abnormal bone or cartilage development but will not suffer slowed growth. And because copper absorption decreases with increased copper intake, symptoms of copper excess have only been noted in horses in experimental situations when very high levels have been fed.

## IRON

FUNCTION: Most of us are familiar with iron's role in hemoglobin, the molecule in red blood cells which enables them to transport oxygen throughout the cells of the body. Approximately 60% of the body's iron is involved in this task, with another 40% incorporated in muscle myoglobin, storage forms, and various enzymes.

SOURCES: The horse's estimated iron needs are about 50 ppm per day for pregnancy and lactation, and growth, and 40 ppm for other mature equines. Most forages contain between 50 and 250 ppm (occasionally, up to 400 ppm) of iron, so under most conditions horses receive plenty of iron in their normal diets.

SIGNS OF DEFICIENCY: Clinically recognized iron deficiencies rarely occur in either foals or mature horses at any perform-ance level. Only under conditions of severe or chronic blood loss is an iron deficiency likely. Sometimes this blood loss is not obvious (it might be the result of a severe intestinal parasite problem, or even a serious case of lice).

If a deficiency does occur, the horse will exhibit impaired performance, followed by anemia (low red blood cell count). Because iron levels are tied to fitness, iron supplements have a reputation for enhancing athletic performance, but they should never be administered unless a blood test has demonstrated actual anemia.

SIGNS OF TOXICITY: Iron toxicosis is far more common in horses than is iron deficiency. Foals are particularly susceptible to iron excesses in the first few days of their lives. Excess iron is stored in various tissues, especially the liver, and severely affected foals (who have usually received inappropriate doses of iron) might suffer depression, dehydration, diarrhea, liver failure, and death. It's important to note that the body has no way to excrete excess iron; its only means of protection is decreased absorption, which works with oral supplements but not with injectables.

High levels of iron might also make him more vulnerable to

bacterial infections. (Bacteria will multiply more efficiently when it is readily available.) Corticosteroids are a source of iron, which is one reason why these drugs might increase a horse's susceptibility to bacterial infections.

## ZINC

FUNCTION: The metabolism of proteins and carbohydrates is assisted by a number of enzymes containing zinc. The absorption of this mineral can vary widely, and it is affected by the level of many other minerals, including copper and iron. Forty ppm of zinc per day has been recommended for adult horses, and a higher level might be beneficial for foals (zinc is considered to play a role in growth and prevention of developmental orthopedic disorders, but to what extent no one is yet sure).

SIGNS OF DEFICIENCY AND TOXICITY: Horses are quite tolerant of high levels of zinc. Zinc toxicosis, resulting from horses grazing in pastures contaminated by zinc smelters or mines, brass foundries, or other industrial plants, has been noted (with symptoms including bony limb deformities, growth plate enlargements, and in severely affected foals, lameness and a strange low-headed, arched-back stance), but it does not occur under normal conditions. Clinical symptoms of zinc deficiency have not been reportedr, though the average level of dietary zinc in most feeds, about 15 ppm, would appear to be inadequate (and is often supplemented by feed companies).

## MANGANESE

FUNCTION: Lipid and carbohydrate metabolism depends on manganese, and this mineral is also essential for the synthesis of the chondroitin sulfate needed for cartilage formation. These are functions involved mostly in reproduction and growth. The exact amount of manganese needed by horses has not yet been determined, though based on other species, 40 ppm per day is generally considered ample.

SIGNS OF DEFICIENCY AND TOXICITY: Although manganese deficiencies are sometimes a problem in ruminants, they have not been described in horses. If such a deficiency did occur, it would likely result in fertility problems in adult breeding stock and in limb deformities in foals. More good news — no harmful level of manganese has been established for horses, which seem to be able to tolerate large quantities of this mineral with no ill effects.

## COBALT

FUNCTION: Cobalt's only known function is as a component of vitamin $B_{12}$ — so a cobalt deficiency results in a $B_{12}$ deficiency. Based on levels recommended for cattle, a minimum of 0.1 ppm of cobalt, and a maximum of 10 ppm, are suggested for horses, but neither deficiencies nor excesses of this mineral (nor of vitamin $B_{12}$) have been described in horses as yet. Most researchers suspect that neither is likely to occur.

### Calcium and Phosphorus Needed by the Horse as Compared to Amount in Common Feeds

| Amount recommended for: | Calcium (% in total diet dry matter) | Phosphorus (% in total diet dry matter) |
|---|---|---|
| Adult maintenance | 0.3 | 0.2 |
| Pregnancy (last three months) and lactation | 0.5 | 0.3 |
| Growth: 1-4 months | 0.8 | 0.5 |
| Growth: 6-12 months | 0.7 | 0.4 |
| Growth: 12-18 months | 0.5 | 0.3 |
| Growth: 18 months-mature | 0.4 | 0.25 |
| Amount present in: Grains | 0.05-0.09 | 0.3-0.4 |
| Wheat bran | 0.1 | 1.3 |
| Grass hay | 0.3-0.5 | 0.1-0.3 |
| Legume hay | 0.8-2.0 | 0.1-0.3 |

# CHAPTER 8

## Hay and Forage

Now that we've discussed at great length the basic components of the equine diet, let's return to the real world, and look at how we can use various foodstuffs to provide an ideal nutritional balance.

We've said it before, we'll say it again: forage should be the basis of any equine diet. So understanding pasture, hay, and other fiber sources — how they're grown, how they're harvested and stored, which are most appropriate for your horse, and how to recognize quality when you see it — is an important part of your everyday management.

Forage can be loosely defined as any feed with a minimum fiber content of 18% and a relatively low dietary energy, or DE, content, made up of the stems, leaves, and stalks of plants. The most natural, least expensive, and safest feed for horses, forage provides the bulk of nutrients horses require for their everyday maintenance metabolism and stimulates the muscle tone and the activity of the gastrointestinal tract. Horses with inadequate amounts of forage in their diets run the risk of colic and founder, as well as stable vices derived from having too little to chew on.

Although horses have been known to nibble on tree leaves and branches, they're primarily grazers, not browsers as deer are, and grasses make up most of their natural diet. If you live in a temperate climate with no chance of drought, your horses might have the luxury of nutritious grazing — fresh forage — year-round. But for most North Americans, there's a good portion of the year when good pasture is just not available, and hay — grasses and/or legumes which have been sun-cured, dried, and baled for convenient feeding — picks up the slack.

Hay, the most common type of forage fed to horses, averages 28% to 38% crude fiber, and has a DE level of about 1.95 to 2.5 Mcal per kg. (Cereal grains, by contrast, contain between 2% and 12% crude fiber, and have a much higher DE, averaging 3.3% to 3.7 Mcal/kg.) Hay is high in calcium and low in phosphorus — and happily, grains are generally high in phosphorus and low in calcium, so a horse being fed both hay and grain usually ingests a Ca:P ratio that "balances out." Hay also contains high levels of potassium and vitamins A, E, and K — and if sun-cured, high levels of vitamin D as well. (Vitamins tend to break down over time, so the more recently the hay was cut, the higher the vitamin content; by the time baled hay is a year old, it may contain no appreciable amount of vitamin A.)

Hay can be extremely variable in protein content. Legume hays (such as alfalfa or clover) might contain 20% crude protein or even higher, while grass hays (such as timothy, Bermuda grass, or orchard grass) average about 11% to 14% protein, and can go as low as 4%. The protein content of hay is largely determined by the time in which it is cut — the younger the hay is, the higher the protein. Hay cut past the mid-bloom stage (when about 50% of the plants have flowered and gone to seed) is a good deal lower in protein

> ## AT A GLANCE
>
> - Forage provides horses with most of the nutrients they need.
>
> - The protein content of hay is largely determined by the time in which it is cut.
>
> - Hay should have a moisture content of less than 20%.
>
> - Moisture-laden hay can pose a fire risk and also invite mold.
>
> - Good quality hay should be green, rather than yellow or brown.

content, and mature (full-bloom or past-bloom) hay might be inadequate to meet an adult horse's nutrient requirements.

There are actually three types of hay, but one type, cereal grain hay, is rarely fed to horses in North America as it is not terribly economical. Cereal grain hay is hay cut from grains such as wheat or barley, while the plant is still green and before the seed is harvested. It is nutritionally similar to grass hay, and the more grain (seeds) the hay contains, the higher its nutritional value. (If the seed heads are lost in harvesting, only straw remains; it makes good bedding but a poor feed.)

Far more common are grass hays and legume hays. Of the legumes, alfalfa, also called lucerne, is the most popular crop; it's estimated that more than half of the hay harvested in the United States is alfalfa, or an alfalfa/grass mix. Other legume hays include clovers (varieties include red, crimson, ladino, and alsike), birdsfoot trefoil, lespedeza, cowpeas, vetch, and even soybeans. Legume hays are almost always preferred by horses over grass hays, and this type contains two to three times the protein and calcium of grasses, as well as more soluble (non-fibrous) carbohydrates, beta-carotene (the precursor of vitamin A), and vitamin E. Because of these qualities, they're the preferred hays for young, growing horses as well as lactating mares. But legumes are generally more costly, and in some parts of North America might be infested with poisonous blister beetles.

There are also a number of different types of grass hay, with timothy being the most widely grown across North America; it's an easy crop to establish on most soils, and tolerates cold well, beginning to grow actively early in the spring, weeks before most other hay crops. But timothy doesn't cope well with extremes of heat and humidity, so in the central and southern United States, growers may turn to alternatives such as quick-curing Coastal Bermuda grass (a variety developed to grow tall enough to harvest as hay, unlike its cousin, common Bermuda, which suits better as a lawn), brome (drought-resistant and hardy, and also cold-tolerant, but less palatable than some other grasses, and so usually grown in combination with alfalfa) or orchard grass (a very drought-resistant species which can be productive even on poor soils). Bluegrass, fescue, reed canarygrass, ryegrass, and Sudan grass are some of the other varieties of grass hays fed to horses. Grass hays not only don't harbor blister beetles, they are often less dusty than legume hays, making them a preferred choice for horses with respiratory problems. And their more modest protein content makes them a better choice than legumes for mature horses not being used for breeding.

You can distinguish a grass hay from a legume by looking at the stalks and leaves: grass hays grow tall, upright stalks and long, slender leaves that sheathe the stalk itself, rather than branching out on stems the way legume leaves do. Legume stalks are often coarser, and the leaves are less firmly attached — which leads to increased wastage after harvest, when the dry leaves tend to shatter and crumble out of the bale. The seed heads of grass hays, however, can vary a great deal, from the narrow, cattail-like structures of timothy, to the branched, tree-like fronds of bluegrass and orchard grass and the elaborate tufts of brome. Some grasses create a thick, underlying carpet of roots and connecting runners called rhizomes, which protect the ground from water runoff and traffic damage; this makes them a preferred crop for pastures.

There are considerable advantages to growing grass and legume hays together as one crop. First, horses consider legumes tops in the palatability sweepstakes, so combining the two might encourage a horse who would turn his nose up at straight grass hay to accept and consume a mixed "flake." Second, a lower-protein grass hay might help "balance out" the high protein level of a legume and create bales which are appropriate to feed to mature horses — and more marketable for the farmer. And third, the addition of nitrogen-producing legumes to a grass hay crop actually helps fertilize the field and increase the yield of the grass hay. In many parts of the North American continent, "mixed" hay is the preferred feed for horses — though the mix may be any of a number of combinations of legumes and grasses, depending on the climate, soil type, and demand.

## HARVESTING AND STORING

The standard method of harvesting hay is to cut the crop and allow it to sun-cure until it has a moisture content of less than 20%, after which it is baled. Growers have to do a delicate dance with the weather, cutting their hay when they hope there is the greatest likelihood of the crop's drying before it is rained on…and sometimes losing the gamble. The

Hay should be cut before mid-bloom.

stage of growth of the hay limits the weather window considerably; in order to ensure good nutritional content, hay should be cut before it reaches the mid-bloom stage. Once seed-heads have formed, the plant puts its energy into propagation, and the stalk and leaves become tougher, more fibrous, and less palatable. The crude protein level of brome grass, for example, might drop from 12.6% (mid-bloom) to 5.6% when fully mature. (Researchers have estimated that allowing hay plants to stand past the "boot" stage, when seed heads first appear, decreases crude protein levels by about 0.25% per day, and digestible energy by nearly 0.50% per day.)

Moisture levels are crucial to hay quality. An ill-timed thunderstorm while hay is curing can reduce the leaf content in the resulting bales by up to 15%, destroy up to 34% of the nonstructural carbohydrates, 25% of the protein yield, and decrease the overall yield of the crop by up to 40%. Baling while the moisture of the hay is still too high (over 20%, or 18% for large rectangular or round bales) increases the chance of mold growth, decreases the protein utilization, and makes the hay less palatable. In addition, hay that is baled wet tends to generate heat (both through the continued respiration of the hay, which can create an environment of 90% to 100% humidity in the bale, and the metabolic activity of microorganisms associated with the

It is best to sun-cure hay until the moisture content is less than 20%.

plant material — including heat-resistant fungi which become active at a temperature between 113 and 150 degrees Fahrenheit). Once these processes are set in motion in baled hay, temperatures can continue to rise through a period of about four to 10 weeks (especially when stored in a warm loft with poor air circulation)...and at temperatures above 175 degrees F, heat-producing chemical reactions serve to worsen the situation further. A subsequent rapid oxidation of reactive compounds in the hay actually can cause the temperature to rise to ignition point — between 448 and 527 degrees F — and if enough oxygen is present, spontaneous combustion might result, not only destroying your hay, but putting your horses and buildings at huge risk.

Bales that feel or smell warm should never be stored anywhere near a barn, and regular checks with a thermometer (slipped down between bales in your stack) are an excellent safety precaution. Hay that heats above 140 degrees F should be removed from the barn — slowly, as even throwing or moving the hay quickly could be enough to cause it to burst into flames. Though regular "square" bales of hay can vary in weight from about 40 to 100 pounds, any unusually heavy bales should be regarded as suspicious — they might have too high a moisture content, and are better discarded.

Heating occurs, to some extent, in all forage materials which contain more than 15% moisture, and many farmers use spray-on drying agents (often containing potassium carbonate), to reduce the risk of baling too wet. The chemicals in the drying agents break down the waxy cuticle layer on the stem, which increases the rate of moisture loss and can cut curing time by 50% to 70%. They also make the leaves less brittle, which results in less leaf (and nutrient) loss.

Check hay for excessive heat.

Another approach is to use a hay preservative, such as propionic acid, which inhibits mold and can allow growers to bale hay at up to 25% moisture. The resulting hay tends to have higher yields, better color, a higher percentage of leaves, and less dust and mildew than conventionally baled hay — not a bad payoff for a chemical that costs about $5 per ton of hay. Both hay preservatives and drying agents have been demonstrated to be safe for use on hay for horses, and have no demonstrated effect on palatability. Their only drawback is that some of the chemicals are corrosive to the growers' equipment. Growers producing large square or round bales often use these products as a precaution against spoilage even when curing conditions are ideal.

Even under the best conditions, hay suffers losses of about 30% to 70% during the harvesting and baling processes, with legumes taking a higher toll than the tougher grasses. Losses from normal respiration account for about 5% or 6% of the total dry matter (and that number can rise if the humidity is high). Another 10% to 25% can be lost in raking and baling. Legume leaves, in particular, can shatter and fall to the ground as they dry, and high leaf loss can significantly compromise the nutritional value, and therefore the quality, of the hay: the leaves of a legume contain about two-thirds of the digestible energy, three-quarters of the protein, and most of the other nutrients.

In warmer regions of North America, growers sometimes are able to get as many as seven or eight cuttings from a hay-field, although in the northern States and Canada two (or at most three) cuttings are the norm. "First-cut" hay is generally high in nutritional value if harvested at the proper time, and runs the lowest risk of blister beetles (which usually appear after midsummer), but sometimes contains large numbers of weeds that have grown up since the last cutting of the previous season. And because it is harvested early in the year, it might be more difficult to get it sun-cured without its being rained on. Later cuttings, in the heat of the summer, have lower nutritional value, because when temperatures are hot, the plants put their energy into rapid growth, with more stem and fewer leaves. But as the weather gets cooler in the fall, hay cuttings usually have a higher leaf and nutrient content, fewer weeds, and, in many areas, the best opportunity of being harvested without rain. Determining the quality of your hay should be based less on which "cut" it is from, than from the stage of bloom it was at when harvested.

## ASSESSING QUALITY

Much of the assessment of the quality of your hay can be done the old-fashioned way: break open a bale and scratch n' sniff! Good quality hay should be green, rather than yellow or brown. (Keep in mind that some hays, particularly some varieties of clover, can cure to quite a dark color, and that this is not necessarily an indicator of mold growth.) It should have a high leaf content ("stemmy" hay is too mature) and few weeds; it should also smell pleasant and slightly sweet. There should be no visible mold (white or dark, matted patches in the hay) or other foreign material. If you take a handful of hay and squeeze it, it should not hurt your hand — prickly hay has been cut too late, and has a low nutrient content. And if you drop a flake of hay from a height of a few feet, you should not see clouds of dust rising from it — dust is usually an indicator that the grower had the tines on his harvester set too low. As a general rule, the nicer you feel that the loose hay would be to sleep in, the better the quality!

To really determine the nutrient content of the hay, however, you'll need to do a hay analysis, as mentioned in Chapter 3. Appearance is a poor indicator of nutritive value — even grass hays that appear very similar can vary in protein content by two to three times. Performing a hay analysis whenever you receive a shipment of hay is an excellent routine to establish, especially as the results may have a significant impact on the grains and supplements you choose to feed.

How much to feed? As a rough guideline, horses should consume 1% to 2% of their bodyweight each day in forage products — at least 50% of their total diets under all but the most extreme exercise programs. Though all of us prefer to feed by "eyeballing" amounts, the weight and size of a flake of hay can vary so much that it is worth weighing the flakes to determine how close you are to these guidelines. This can be done very simply by standing on a bathroom scale, with and without the flake of hay, and subtracting the difference.

When feeding hay, it's important to remember that, at heart, horses are grazing animals, programmed to chew on stemmy, fibrous plants for at least 12 hours a day. That urge to chew can be almost as compelling as a rodent's, so hay fulfills two functions in your barn: it provides nutrients (and keeps the digestive system in good health), but it also keeps horses busy (and thus not chewing the wood fences, stall doors, or their neighbor's tails!). An almost constant supply of small amounts of hay is far more beneficial than one or two large feedings a day, because it mimics the horse's natural grazing habits. Make lots of good-quality hay the basis of your horses' diets, and you'll reap the benefits in terms of both health and contentment.

## A FEW ALTERNATIVES

Though regular baled hay is the mainstay of equine diets across North America, it's not the only forage option. Hay also can be pressed into cubes, chopped and processed into pellets, or fermented as silage or "haylage." If your horse suffers from chronic respiratory allergies (such as Chronic Obstructive Pulmonary Disease, also called "broken wind" or "heaves"), has dental troubles which make chewing hay diffi-cult, or is very elderly, one of these alternative forms of forage might be just the ticket.

Hay cubes and pellets are simply hay which has been chopped coarsely or finely and formed (with the addition of a binder) into scoopable, baggable pieces. They're more con-venient to move around than baled hay, and have the advan-tage of a guaranteed nutritional content, posted on the bag — so you'll know exactly what you're delivering in terms of nutrients. Hay cubes and pellets come in a variety of sizes and textures, from soft and crumbly to quite hard, and they might be all-alfalfa, all-grass hay, a mixture of the two, or even hay mixed with other prod-

**Pellets are an alternative to hay.**

ucts such as ground corn cobs. Hard, crunchy products are generally preferred by horses, but if you are feeding a toothless octogenarian, for example, you can easily soak hay cubes or pellets in a bit of water to make them easier to consume. Soaked or unsoaked, these processed hay products have a significant advantage over regular hay for an allergic horse: they are many times less dusty than even the highest-quality baled forage (even so, be sure to sort out the fines in the bottom of the bag). Some horses with chronic heaves can become almost symptomless when, along with other management changes to minimize dust, hay is eliminated from the diet in favor of hay cubes or pellets.

The down side of processed hay products? There are really only three. The first is that, unlike a hay bale you can crack open and examine, it can be difficult to assess the quality of the forage used to make the product. Despite the guaranteed analysis on the feed tag, it's impossible to tell whether weeds, dirt, or other contaminants have been incorporated into the cubes or pellets. The best advice is to buy from a reputable company, and look for pieces of a uniform color and texture, with a pleasant smell. This brings us to the second disadvantage of processed hay products: they are usually considerably more expensive than ordinary hay. However, it's very true in the feed business that you get what you pay for, so pass over the most inexpensive hay cube or pellet you see in favor of a better-quality feed which likely will have a higher price tag. The difference will be worth it in terms of peace of mind.

Finally, the convenient shape of hay cubes or pellets can in itself be a disadvantage. Because they take less time to chew than regular hay, horses generally consume them faster — and that sometimes leaves them with a dissatisfied chewing urge. Be prepared for the possibility of boredom-based destructive behaviors as a result.

The other alternative form of hay is usually called haylage, or sometimes, "horsehage." This is hay harvested at its nutritive best, then stored in anaerobic conditions while still at a relatively high moisture content. It is often treated as a dry silage — that is, the hay is baled as usual (often in large round bales) and then coated in heavy plastic to encourage fermentation. If properly done, ensiling ensures that the hay retains its nutrients much better than it would have if sun-cured; it maintains high levels of protein, carbohydrates, carotene, and many vitamins better than any other method of feed preservation. (Because haylage is not exposed to the sun, however, it is lower in vitamin D than naturally cured hay.)

When anaerobic conditions are maintained correctly while making haylage, molds, yeasts, and aerobic bacteria perish while anaerobic microorganisms present in the hay ferment the soluble carbohydrates, producing lactic and volatile fatty acids. In fact, the process mimics what happens in the horse's own cecum and colon when forage is digested. The acids inhibit microbial growth, eventually stopping the fermentation after several weeks. The moisture content of the feed must be monitored carefully, as too high or too low a level might allow excess heat to be generated (which results in spoilage), or the growth of yeasts, molds, and toxic bacteria.

Good haylage should have a clean, pleasant acid odor, is uniform in color — green to brownish — and feels moist, but not mushy or slimy. Dark brown, caramelized, or charred-looking or -smelling feed is a sign that excessive heating occurred during fermentation, and black patches indicate it is rotten. Haylage like this should obviously not be fed. Likewise, anything with an unpleasant or sharp odor should be tossed out. Healthy haylage should have a pH of 3.5 to 5.0 (this can easily be tested with a pH strip). Botulism, a potentially toxic anaerobic bacterium, is a particular risk with haylage. It can brew in any bale with a pH over 4.5. Because the plastic covering protects the haylage from microbial growth, any feed in plastic which has been ripped or punctured should be discarded. Once you do open a package, feed the haylage within a couple of days at maximum.

Despite the greater care it requires, many horsepeople

prefer haylage to traditional sun-cured bales, citing its extremely good palatability (most horses, once familiar with it, strongly prefer it to regular hay), its superior nutritive value, its almost dust-free qualities (making it another good choice for a horse with COPD), and the lack of wastage. Because its moisture content is higher than that of hay, however, it may take two to three times as much haylage to replace each flake of hay.

Next, we'll have a look at the many types of grains available.

## Hay Nutrient Content for Horses

| Hay Type | DE (Mcal /kg) | Crude Protein (%) | Crude Fiber (%) | Calcium (%) | Phosphorus (%) | Vitamin A (IU/kg x1000) | Vitamin E (mg/kg) |
|---|---|---|---|---|---|---|---|
| Legume - early bloom | 2.4 | 17 - 20 | 21 - 30 | 1.0 - 1.8 | 0.1 - 0.3 | 50 - 85 | 20 - 40 |
| Legume - full bloom | 2.1 | 15 - 18 | 32 | 1.0 - 1.9 | 0.1 - 0.3 | 10 - 30 | 10 - 20 |
| Grass - early bloom | 2.1 | 11 - 14 | 30 - 34 | 0.3 - 0.5 | 0.1 - 0.3 | 15 - 25 | 10 - 30 |
| Grass - mature | 1.8 | 6 - 10 | 32 - 36 | 0.3 - 0.5 | 0.1 - 0.3 | 5 - 15 | |
| Cereal grains, cut green | 1.9 | 9 | 29 | 0.15 - 0.35 | 0.1 - 0.3 | 10 - 35 | |

# CHAPTER 9
## *Grains*

It's five p.m., and up and down the aisle of a large boarding stable, the nickering, rumbling, and pawing begin. What's the cause of the excitement? Nothing more than a metal scoop digging into a bin of grain, a sound that tips off every equine resident that it's dinner time. Hay seldom receives this sort of reception; it's grain that horses really relish.

But just because horses love grain doesn't mean it's an essential part of the diet. In a wild state, they encounter grain only as an occasional plant seedhead — certainly never in the volumes found in their feed buckets in a domestic scenario. While their teeth can grind grain seeds quite efficiently, their digestive systems are poorly equipped to deal with the low-fiber, high-carbohydrate wallop that grain delivers, thus the much higher incidence of colic among grain-fed horses compared with those fed only forages.

As most of us know, the intake of an excess quantity of any type of grain can result in dire consequences, including life-threatening colic and founder. Unfortunately for them, equines have no dietary wisdom when it comes to grain, and given the opportunity to gorge themselves (if for instance, the feed room door is left open), they can conceivably eat themselves to death. Because of this, grain should never be fed free-choice or left so that it is accessible to horses outside of their allotted amount at mealtimes. And except in some very exceptional circumstances (largely, horses in hard race training), the grain portion should never be more than 50%, by weight, of a horse's total daily ration. It need not be fed at all, in fact, unless you wish to supplement the energy or nutrient demands of your horses beyond what their forage provides. A good many pleasure horses, especially those who are "easy keepers," do very nicely without the addition of grain to their diets.

> ## AT A GLANCE
>
> • The grain portion of a horse's diet should never exceed 50%, by weight, of the horse's total daily ration.
>
> • Too much grain can disrupt the digestive system.
>
> • Oats, corn, and mixed feeds are the most common types of grains.
>
> • Pelleted and extriuded feeds provide an alternative to traditional grains.

Grains in their natural state supply very little in the way of vitamins (commercially mixed rations are generally vitamin supplemented), but they do provide an important mineral that might be lacking in a horse on a forage-only diet: phosphorus. Hay and pasture provide generous amounts of the macromineral calcium, but an inadequate amount of phosphorus. Both of these minerals are crucial to correct bone and muscle development and maintenance, and the ratio between them in the horse's diet is pivotal (as we saw in Chapter 7). Too little phosphorus, and bone-building and repair are not carried out as they should be; too much, and the whole system is out of balance and seeks to re-establish it by leaching existing calcium out of the bone, eventually causing bone abnormalities. So grains, which are generally high in phosphorus and low in calcium, can make the perfect companion to hay because when both are fed in the correct quantities, they provide an almost ideal Ca:P ratio for the horse.

An individual grain is actually the seedhead of the plant, containing the nutrient store for the germ (embryo) from which a new plant develops. It consists of a coat, a starchy endosperm, and the germ itself. Some grains, such as barley, rice, oats, and husked sorghum (milo) have a fused husk or hull, which provides extra fiber; others, such as corn, wheat, rye, and millet, do not.

The grains that are fed to horses vary greatly from continent to continent. In North America and parts of Europe, oats and corn are the most popular, but milo (sorghum) is commonly fed to all types of livestock in Central America, and wheat (despite its low palatability) is used in many parts of the world. Even relatively obscure grains, like triticale, spelt, and emmer have found their way into the diets of horses.

Oats (*Avena sativa*) are the traditional favorite, reported to make up more than 30% of all commercially prepared horse feeds. The same quality that makes them such a popular feed for horses is responsible for their being less favored for other livestock: they have a low energy density compared to most other grains. That's a result of the fibrous hull, which makes

**Horses seem to prefer oats.**

up a significant portion of the oat seed and makes oats a "safer" feed for horses (less likely to cause cecal acidosis, because of a lower starch content) than hull-less grains such as corn and wheat.

Horses also seem to prefer oats over most other grains, making them a close second in the palatability sweepstakes to molasses-laced sweet feeds. But oats tend to vary more both in quality and price than most other grain crops, and the yield per acre is relatively low. Their popularity with owners and trainers, in many cases, seems to have more to do with habit, and a lack of familiarity with other cereal grains, than anything else.

Because oats have a relatively soft kernel, most adult horses have no difficulty chewing and digesting them. Oats can be "clipped" (a process in which the pointed top and tail of the grain are clipped off), "crimped" (lightly crushed so as to crack, but not completely remove, the hull), or rolled (to make oatmeal), but these processing techniques are rarely needed to make oats a good horse feed, except in the case of very young or very old equines, or those with tooth problems.

Oats have the advantage of being less vulnerable to molds and mycotoxins than most other grains. But because of their relatively small growing area (they grow best in cool weather, limiting their cultivation to the northern States and southern Canada) and low yields, oats are becoming less and less popular as a major crop — which means that oats are more expensive than other grains, and likely to become more so.

It pays to shop for good quality, "heavy" oats (sometimes called "racehorse oats") because they contain less foreign material and weigh more per unit of volume. The individual grains should look plump, light blonde in color, and fairly uniform in size. Slimmer, lightweight oats may provide the same nutrition, but less value for your dollar.

Dehulled oats, sometimes called groats, are an alternative feed sometimes available for horses. They provide more digestible energy per pound, but lack the safety margin that the oat hull provides. That, coupled with the high cost of processing the grains this way, makes groats a far less popular feed for horses than they were in the past.

Corn (*Zea mays*), or maize, as it's known in many parts of the world, is probably the second most familiar grain for horses, and overall as a livestock feed, it is the leading crop in the United States. It constitutes more than 80% of the grain fed to animals in North America, and its production continues to rise. Most horses find it only slightly less palatable than oats, and more tasty than many other cereal grains, and it is a good-quality and nutritious grain for horses.

Because corn is a hull-less grain, however, it is very high in starches. Fiber makes up only 2.2% of its total composition, and its digestible energy (DE) value is more than twice that of oats. This means that it does not have the "safety margin" that oats enjoy, and it must be fed with caution and in relatively small quantities. Many nutritionists recommend against corn's being fed as the sole grain for this reason, suggesting that it is best mixed with other grains to balance its high starch concentration.

Corn's reputation for being a feed that makes horses "hot" and hard to handle is largely a myth; it stems from owners who have carelessly substituted corn for an equal quantity of oats in their horse's diets — unwittingly supplying more than twice the energy! Feeding by weight, rather than by volume, is crucial when switching grains.

**Corn is a good-quality, nutritious grain.**

The hardness of the individual kernels means that in order to be digested well by the horse, corn usually needs to be processed, by cracking (breaking each kernel into pieces), or flaking (flattening kernels with a roller). That processing increases the utilization of the grain, but also exposes it to the possible growth of molds and mycotoxins which can cause aflatoxicosis and moldy corn disease (both potentially fatal) if ingested. Of all the cereal grains fed to horses, corn is the most likely to be contaminated by molds, particularly if poorly stored (in very damp, humid, or hot conditions). Because of this, any corn that is even remotely questionable should never be fed.

But contrary to popular belief, corn is not a "heating" feed in the traditional sense. In fact, because the greatest amount of internal heat in the horse's body is generated through the microbial fermentation of fiber, not starches, increasing the amount of hay in your horse's diet in winter will generate more body heat than will increasing the amount of corn he eats. However, because corn provides lots of energy per pound, and energy needs increase during cold weather, corn is a good winter feed for horses.

Very popular in the United Kingdom and Europe as a horse feed, barley (*Hordeum vulgare*) doesn't enjoy the same favor on this side of the Atlantic. However, it has a long and honored history on the equine bill of fare, even being reputed to have been the staple diet for the early Arabian herds who laid the foundation for so many modern horse breeds. Today, it's the most widely cultivated cereal grain in the world, needing a shorter growing season than corn and tolerating limited rainfall well. Over half of the world's harvest of barley comes from Europe and the former Soviet Union. In the United States, about half of the total barley crop (only about one-twentieth of the corn harvest) is fed to livestock, with another 25% going towards alcohol production.

Barley grains resemble smallish oats, but are harder. Because of this, they usually are rolled or crimped when fed to horses. (In the UK, it's common to cook the barley grains, making the starches more digestible and the meal far more palatable.) Processed barley can be dusty, and if finely ground, the end product, which is heavy and low in bulk, might tend to pack in the stomach and present a colic risk. For this reason, when barley is fed as the principal grain, it's often mixed with a fibrous product such as chopped hay or straw (chaff), or beet pulp, to keep the digestive system moving everything along. It's also used as a major component in commercial pelleted feeds.

Like oats, most types of barley contain hulls, providing the grain with a higher fiber content than corn, but lower than oats. In fact, barley could be described as an "in-between" grain in many ways — supplying more digestible energy and total digestible nutrients (TDN) than the same quantity of oats, but not as much as corn — and between oats and corn in terms of fiber content and "safety," as well as heat produced in its digestion. But it's slightly higher in protein than either oats or corn (making it a good choice for breeding stock and young horses), has a very high phosphorus content (so high, in fact, that it is undesirable as a single grain even when fed with high-calcium alfalfa to balance it out), and less of its starch tends to be processed in the small intestine, increasing the risk of cecal acidosis. In addition, barley is less palatable than oats and corn, and is most commonly used in a grain mix with oats, corn, and frequently molasses.

Grain sorghum, or milo (*S. vulgare*), represents about 6% to 8% of the grain fed to livestock in the United States, and it can make a good feed for horses, though its feed value varies depending on its tannin content. Tannins provide a degree of resistance to mold, but decrease milo's protein digestibility and palatability, as well as giving it an astringent taste. Brown milo, which has the highest concentration of tannins, is not a suitable feed for horses because of this. (Unfortunately, yellow milo, the preferred variety, is often difficult to differentiate from brown, visually.)

Milo has a small, hard kernel, and for efficient use by horses, it must be steam-flaked. Whole grains, or even those that have been dry rolled, are too difficult for horses to chew and digest. Like corn, milo is high in energy density and low in fiber, so it must be fed with caution.

Wheat, rye, and even hulled rice all can make suitable additions to the horse's diet in addition to the grains described above, but they seldom are fed in North America, usually either because their palatability is low or because their cost and/or availability are prohibitive. However, they occasionally make an appearance on the feed label of a commercially mixed ration.

## PROCESSING GRAINS

The practice of processing grains sometimes can markedly improve their digestibility, but it is not without its disadvantages. Chief among these is the fact that when you break the hard coat that is the seed's natural protection, you make it vulnerable to invasion from microorganisms as well as insects. You also open the endosperm to more rapid nutrient breakdown on exposure to the elements. At the very least, breaking open the kernel exposes the grain to oxidation, causing a stale flavor which quickly decreases its palatability. (Some feed companies apply antioxidants and mold inhibitors to their processed grains to combat this.) Grains which have been crimped, rolled, steamed, or otherwise processed must be stored for much shorter periods than whole grains, and must be watched closely for signs of mold.

In the case of oats, no increase in feeding value has been noted for processed (crimped, rolled, or steam flaked) oats vs. whole grains — and most nutritionists recommend that oats only be processed for those horses with dental problems. But in the case of harder grains, such as barley and corn, processing can provide significant advantages in terms of the amount of starch digested in the small intestine (as opposed to the cecum), and reduce the risk of diarrhea, colic, and founder. For small hard grains, such as milo, rye, and wheat, processing is essential for horses to extract any nutrient value.

Methods of processing can include cracking and rolling of the dry grains to varying degrees. The grains should not be finely ground, as this decreases palatability and increases the dustiness of the ration; in addition, some researchers suspect it might contribute to gastric ulcers as it does in pigs. In any case, the use of finely ground grain is no better (and possibly worse) than more coarsely ground kernels. Larger pieces of the individual kernels also make it easier for you to assess the quality of the grain.

Heat processing, which can include steam-flaking, micronizing, pelleting, and extruding almost invariably makes grain more expensive, but it also offers some pluses. Studies have shown that protein use from both oats and milo is 2% to 3% higher when these grains are micronized (cooked with dry-heat microwaves), and starch digestion of corn in the small intestine was improved by almost three times when the grain was extruded. In addition, most horses show a marked preference for processed grains over unprocessed ones, in the case of every grain except oats.

## WHICH TO BUY?

Although all of the grains discussed here can have a valuable place in your horse's diet, no single grain will provide all the nutrients a working horse needs, even when fed in combination with premium-quality hay. Of all the grains commonly fed to horses, oats are generally considered the closest to the "perfect" feed, but even oats fail to supply sufficient quantities of many vitamins and minerals, and their relative energy density is low (which as we know, makes them safer but more expensive to feed, pound per pound).

This is the point where commercially balanced rations offer a tremendous advantage. Formulated with a mix of grains, and generally supplemented with a mixture of vitamins and minerals appropriate to the type of horse it is designed for (i.e. performance horses, breeding stock, or growing youngsters), a commercial ration provides what no single grain can: balanced nutrition. Commercially prepared feeds take a lot of the guesswork out of calculating whether your horse is receiving all the vitamins and minerals he needs. Feed companies employ Ph.D. nutritionists to formulate such feeds, and the end result is a ration that needs no added powders or potions to provide complete nutrition.

You can, of course, also do your own calculations and create your own balanced feed from a mixture of grains, but the math can sometimes be daunting, and the results dependent on how complete your understanding of nutrition is. However, it's comforting to know that from crop to crop, the nutrient values listed in charts like the one on page 125 are far more reliable for grain than for hay (the content of which can fluctuate wildly depending on the soil, growing conditions, and season). If you are interested in formulating your own ration, consult your feed company's equine specialist or your state extension specialist (whom you can locate by contacting the nearest university with an agricultural college). He or she can help provide you with reliable information on how to tailor a grain ration to your horse's needs.

The most popular format for a mixed feed is what the feed industry calls a "textured ration," and what most of us know as "sweet feed." Sweet feed is simply a mixture of grains, with a touch of sweet flavoring, usually molasses, added to improve palatability, reduce dustiness, and bind the mixture. Within that description, there's room for an infinite number of variations, depending on the ingredients used. Some sweet feeds are basic in the extreme, while others feature lots of nutritional bells and whistles — a pumped-up vitamin and mineral supplement, perhaps some added fats and oils, and/or extra fiber, in the form of dehydrated alfalfa or shredded beet pulp. To prevent spoilage, most

Sweet feed is the most popular format for a mixed feed.

sweet feeds also include a preservative. The chemical-phobic can take heart, however: often, the feed industry uses a natural anti-oxidant, such as vitamin E, to do the job.

When selecting a sweet feed, use all of your senses. Look for healthy, plump individual grains in the mix, a pleasantly sweet smell, and very little in the way of dust or fines. Most sweet feeds have a shelf life of about six months (or three months if fat-supplemented), but any sign of moldiness or insect contamination means the feed should be discarded. Generally, beware of feeds which have very heavy molasses — not only is such a mix very difficult to work with, sticking to everything in summer and freezing solid in the winter, but it is more prone to spoilage. In addition, molasses can very well disguise inferior ingredients and a high dust content. It is often a sign of a multitude of sins being committed at the feed mill! You are better to pay a little more for a feed with high-quality ingredients that don't need camouflage.

## PELLETED FEEDS

Almost as familiar a sight in the average feed room as sweet feed, is a bag of small, cylindrical shapes called pellets. Pelleting, a versatile technology, is used for everything from rabbit feed to parrot and monkey chow...and it's been a popular option for horse rations for many years now.

Granted, pelleted feeds don't usually exude the tempting aroma that most molasses-laced sweet feeds have, but they more than make up for that in terms of convenience and digestibility. Feed mills have learned to apply pelleting techniques to practically every type of feed a horse can consume, from hay to grains to combinations of the two (often called "complete" feeds). Almost no commercial feed ration is left untouched by the pelleting process — sift through a prepared sweet feed with your fingers, and you'll likely discover a smattering of pellets mixed in with the oats and corn and other grains. That pellet generally contains a vitamin/mineral supplement for the ration, bound up with a fibre source such as dehydrated alfalfa.

Pellets are made by first grinding the grain into particles of a uniform size — not too fine, and not too coarse. The particles then are combined with a "binder," for horse feed. Most companies use natural binders as much as possible — wheat, in particular, is an excellent binder, which helps make a hard, durable pellet, and barley also does a creditable job. So does molasses, a naturally sticky product which does double duty as a flavoring agent.

In the case of a recipe which has little in the way of ingredients that are natural binders, manufacturers may add an artificial binder, usually a product called "lignasol," which is a fine yellow powder. Widely used in other livestock feeds because it is less expensive than natural binders, and because it is easy to work with, lignasol has a limited use in horse feeds because there is a consumer perception that "natural" is better — and horse feed recipes are far more driven by consumer opinion than are, for instance, cattle feeds.

In a mixing chamber, the ground particles are churned together and compacted, and the binder is mixed through (except in the case of a "wet" binder like molasses, which is generally added during "conditioning," the next step in the process). Then the particles move on to a "pellet mill conditioner," where forced steam heats them to a temperature of 180 to 190 degrees Fahrenheit, for about 20 seconds. (Longer exposure to the steam has been found to make a more durable pellet, so some newer mills are now equipped with "double pass" steaming chambers, a process which steams the ingredients twice.) Steaming gelatinizes the starches in the grain, which makes it stick together, and helps it slip through the die (metal plate with holes that create the pellet shape) better. The object is not to cook the grain, which would destroy vitamins and minerals, but just to break the bonds in the complex starches; some researchers feel this increases the overall digestibility of the grain as well. (Increased digestibility of gelatinized starches has been demonstrated in dogs, cats, pigs, and poultry, but the jury is still out with regard to ruminants and horses.)

The next step is pushing the feed (at relatively low pressure) through the die. The size of the holes determines the size of the resulting pellet, and many manufacturers attempt to mark their products with a pellet of distinct dimensions, anywhere from about the thickness of a pencil to about the thickness of your thumb. Pelleted products designed for foals are sometimes finer than those made for adult horses.

The pellets then drop into a pellet mill cooler, where excess moisture is drawn out until the product contains less than 15.5% moisture overall. This step is essential to prevent mold growth. Once it is accomplished, pelleted feeds have little chance of going moldy unless they are stored in damp conditions. Before bagging, the pellets undergo one final step in their journey through the mill when they travel through a pellet shaker, a device like a giant sifter which removes the small chips and fines from the intact pellets and recycles them into the next batch.

A number of factors determine how hard and durable, or how soft and crumbly, a pellet is, including the amount of exposure to steam, the retention time in the die, moisture levels in the feed, the ambient temperature and humidity, and the type and amount of the binder. Feed mills can now actually measure the relative durability of a pellet. If the durability is unacceptable, the feed is recycled and reprocessed. Not only does a soft pellet tend to be dusty, it's generally considered less toothsome to horses, who show a marked preference for harder, crunchier pellets as a rule.

### Advantages of pelleted feeds include the following:

• Pelleted feeds are significantly less dusty than unprocessed grains. This can be an important factor if you are feeding a horse with respiratory problems. Because pellets are not coated with molasses, as are most commercial sweet feeds, they are also easier to handle in the winter.

• Horses can't sort ingredients in a pelleted feed. If you have a picky eater who likes to sort all the oats out of his sweet feed and leave the rest, he is likely not getting the nutrition the ration is designed to deliver. With a pellet, he has no choice but to eat the whole thing. The unpleasant taste or texture of some ingredients, such as fats and oils, can also be "disguised" in a pelleted ration and ingested more readily than they would if top-dressed.

• Because pellets are relatively low in moisture, feeding them tends to result in reduced manure output — especially in the case of hay pellets. The advantages of this need hardly be explained to anyone who has ever wielded a muck fork! Some researchers feel, however, that this may increase the risk of impaction in some horses; studies are currently examining the question.

• Because pellets are made up of feed ground into particles, they are, in a manner of speaking "pre-chewed." This makes them a much more digestible choice than whole grains or hay for very young or old horses, or for any horse with a mouth or tooth problem. Pellets can also be soaked into a mush to be fed to elderly horses who have little or no grinding surfaces left on their teeth. (Pellets have not been shown to increase overall digestibility of a ration when fed to adult horses with no chewing difficulties, however.)

### Disadvantages:

• Some researchers feel that since horses tend to eat pellets more quickly than unprocessed feeds, this format also might increase the risk of digestive upset, as the finer particles can have a tendency to pack in the gut. However, studies have demonstrated no difference in the rate of intestinal fermentation between sweet feeds and pelleted feeds — an argument against an increased risk of colic. These results are still open to interpretation.

• Because they are compacted and bulky, pellets can carry a slightly increased risk of choke, especially in horses who bolt their feed. Strategies to help address this problem include placing a few large, smooth stones in the feed tub; feeding little and often; mixing in some chaff, chopped hay, or soaked beet pulp; and placing some bars across the feed tub, similar to a foal feeder. Or try this: Choose smallish pellets and spread them out thinly in a large, shallow feed tub to make your horse slow down and work for his meal.

• It can be difficult to assess the quality of a pelleted product, because the ingredients are compacted and ground. The manufacturer's nutritional analysis (printed on the bag or on a feed tag attached to the product) should provide you with some assurance, but the only way to be sure of the quality of a pelleted ration is to examine it visually for a firm (not crumbly) texture, a pleasant smell, no visible signs of mold, weeds, or foreign material, and few fines (small dusty particles)… and to send a sample of the product for a nutritional analysis by a commercial or university laboratory. Buying from a reputable manufacturer which offers a product guarantee can go a long way toward your peace of mind.

• The cost of processing a grain pellet will almost always push the price of such a ration up past what unprocessed feeds would cost.

## EXTRUDED FEEDS

A more recent addition to the world of horse feeds is the extruded feed. Extruded products look like dog kibble (they're made by the same process). They're largish, spherical, lightweight pieces of uniform color, hard and somewhat crunchy in texture. In the United Kingdom, they are sometimes called "pony nuts." Extruded products are made by the same basic process that produces pellets, with one important difference: the mix is forced through the die openings under high pressure. When the feed emerges from the die, the sudden release of this pressure causes the particles to expand, almost like popping corn. As a result, extruded products are about half as dense as pelleted products or sweet feeds made with the same ingredients.

Because extruded feeds are made up of fairly large individual particles, they take longer for a horse to chew. This can be a significant advantage for horses who tend to bolt their feed, or colic easily. However, many horses find the shape and texture strange at first. They might require some time to become accustomed to it. And because the "kernels" of extruded feeds are less dense, you get less feed value per bag — often at the same price. Still, extruded products are very spoilage-resistant, and many horses seem to maintain their weight well on them, making them a popular choice.

Whatever the format, when you buy grain, trust your senses. If it doesn't look or smell palatable to you, you probably don't want to feed it to your horses. Buy only the best-quality grain you can afford, buy it in small quantities whenever possible to ensure freshness, and store it properly.

## Comparative Values for Grains Commonly Fed to Horses

| Grain | Relative Feeding Value by volume (%) | Decrease in density if ground | Crude Protein (%) | Crude Fiber (%) | Comments |
|---|---|---|---|---|---|
| Oats (regular) | 45 | 28 | 11 - 12 | 11 | Most palatable and safest grain — often most expensive and variable in quality. |
| Oats (heavy) | 50 | 28 | 12.5 | 11 | Also called "race horse" or "jockey" oats |
| Groats (hull-less oats) | 95 | 18 | 2.4 | | |
| Corn (maize) | 100 | 14 | 8 - 10 | 2.2 | Grain most prone to mold and most commonly overfed. |
| Barley | 85 | 25 | 12 | 5 | Between oats and corn in safety, but less palatable. |
| Sorghum (milo) | 95 | | 11.5 | 2.6 | Should be processed. Brown variety is high-tannin, less digestible and less palatable. |
| Wheat | 110 | 14 | 11 - 14 | 1.5 - 3 | Less palatable than corn or oats. Should be processed. |
| Rye | 100 | 14 | 12 | 2.2 | Feed processed, with 1/3 maximum in grain mix. Ensure no ergot (a poisonous fungus). |
| Wheat bran | | | 16-17 | 10-12 | Not a laxative. When fed, ensure there is as much Ca as P in the total diet |
| Rice bran | | | 14 | 13 | Fed as a fat supplement (fat content 15% dry matter). Ca:P imbalance similar to wheat bran. |

# CHAPTER 10

## Ration Balancing

Here's where we put it all together. It's time to take all of that information from our preceding chapters, and formulate some balanced diets for our horses. This is where most people freeze in fear!

Relax. It's true that there are all sorts of complicated calculations you can do to determine optimum levels of every essential nutrient, but it's also true that, 90% of the time, you don't need to perform any convoluted math to ensure your equines' good health. Your horse will tell you if he's receiving good nutrition — by his shiny coat, good appetite, pleasant outlook, and appropriate energy level. If you are feeding average-to-excellent quality forage and grain, you can be reasonably assured that your horse's diet will meet his daily nutrient requirements. This is nearly always the case when you feed a commercial ration without supplements; and only during growth (especially in the first year), lactation, and the last three months of pregnancy are horses likely to need extra nutritional support. Supplementing also might be necessary if the forage you're feeding is of poor quality (assuming, of course, that you're unable to replace it with something better).

It's worth noting, however, that contrary to popular belief, horses do *not* have "nutritional wisdom" when it comes to their diets. Some marketing pros would have you believe that horses instinctively choose the plants and nutrients they need for good health. Alas, that's not the case — if it were true, we would never have a problem with horses gorging themselves with grain till they colic. With the exception of salt and water, horses do not develop cravings for the nutrients they require; they simply function according to appetite and taste preference, just as we do.

A horse's daily menu needs to include about 40 different nutrients in all: the proper amounts of energy and protein, 15 different minerals, plus chlorine, 14 different vitamins, plus beta carotene, fat, water, and at least four amino acids (lysine, methionine, tryptophane, and threonine). Fortunately, as we know, most of these are known to be provided in adequate amounts by any common equine diet. The only ones which might be inadequate or excessive are: protein, digestible energy (DE), calcium, phosphorus, and selenium. For growing horses, add zinc and copper to that list; for adult horses, the levels of these two minerals is generally adequate in any diet. Levels of vitamins A and E also can be a concern for growing horses and those in high-performance situations in the winter months when they have no access to growing forage. So it's only these nutrients which need to be taken into consideration when formulating a ration.

Before you get out your calculator, you need to know a few basic things:

1) What stage of life is your horse in? Are you feeding a growing foal, a lactating broodmare, an adult pleasure horse, or a hundred-mile endurance champion? This will have an im-

---

## AT A GLANCE

- A horse's daily menu should include about 40 different nutrients.

- The total weight of feed per day should be between 1.5% and 3.0% of a horse's body weight.

- A horse's nutritional needs depend on the type of work he does.

- There are several methods, besides a scale, of determining a horse's weight.

---

portant bearing on the nutrients required.

2) Is your horse idle, or doing work of light, medium, or serious intensity? Is his workload due to be increased, decreased, or remain constant?

3) Is your horse in the condition you'd like him to be in? Is he too fat, or too thin? (See the chart on page 142 to "condition score" your horse. The ideal is a '5'.)

4) What feeds are available to you? Which are reasonably priced? There is no use formulating a ration which is based on ingredients you can't get, or which are outrageously expensive.

Next, you need to know your horse's body weight. The most accurate way to do this is to stand him on a scale specifically designed for horses, but you'll likely only have access to this equipment if you are lucky enough to live nearby a university veterinary school. A rough approximation of your horse's weight can be obtained by using the "heart-girth" measuring tapes sold at many feed stores for a couple of dollars, though these are sometimes "off" by more than a hundred pounds (and incidentally, are useless for pregnant mares, whose heartgirth alone will not tell the story). A more accurate result can be obtained by using the following relatively simple formula:

$$\text{Bodyweight in lbs.} = \frac{[\text{(heartgirth in inches)}^2 \times \text{length in inches}]}{330}$$

where the length of your horse is measured from the front point of his shoulder-blade to the point of his rump.

If you prefer to do Metric calculations, use:

$$\text{Bodyweight in kg} = \frac{[\text{(heartgirth in cm)}^2 \times \text{length in cm}]}{11{,}880}$$

For light-horse foals one to six weeks of age, use:

$$\text{Bodyweight in lbs.} = \frac{[\text{heartgirth in inches} - 25.1]}{0.07}$$

OR

Bodyweight in kg = $\dfrac{\text{[heartgirth in cm} - 63.7]}{0.38}$.

It's worth doing these calculations, because once you have your horse's weight, there's a simple rule of thumb you can use to determine how much feed your horse should be getting each day. The total weight of feed per day should be between 1.5% and 3.0% of your horse's body weight.

Using this rule, a 950-pound Morgan gelding (for example) would need between 14.25 pounds and 28.5 pounds of total feed (forage plus grain). That's a good bit of leeway, of course, and it allows some adjustability. For example, if our Morgan was overweight and only in light work, you would lean toward the lower end of the scale, at 14.25 pounds a day. If, on the other hand, he was in top physical condition and was competing in a high-intensity sport like endurance racing or upper-level combined driving, he might require closer to 28 pounds of feed a day to provide him with the energy he needs.

The 1.5% to 3.0% rule works for almost all types of horses, except for nursing foals (who will only eat between 0.5% to 0.75% of their bodyweight in solid food while they are nursing) and weanlings, who might consume up to 3.5% of their bodyweight per day. The chart on page 143 shows how the intake will vary depending on the horse's activity and energy requirements. Intense work, lactation (nursing), and growth all need to be fueled by larger amounts of nutrients. To some extent, the intake will also be affected by temperament (laid-back, easy keepers will be at the lower end of the scale, while nervous or high-strung horses who are hard keepers will need more), and climate (because it takes more energy to maintain internal body temperature in below-freezing weather).

In order to use the rule effectively, you will have to weigh your horse's feed. Most horsemen, of course, don't operate this systematically — we're used to just estimating by the 'coffee-can' method of measuring (this horse gets half a scoop, this one a whole scoop, that pony a handful). Rest assured that weighing the ration need not be a daily routine — once you've done it a few times, you should be able to estimate by eye fairly effectively. But it's important to weigh both the hay and the grain your horse receives at least a few times; otherwise your guesstimates might not be very accurate.

Hay bales can vary in weight from under 40 pounds to more than 100 pounds. They also vary in terms of the number of flakes they contain. The simplest way to determine their weight is to bring your bathroom scale out to the barn. Stand on it empty-handed to find your own weight, then repeat the process while hoisting a bale of hay. Subtract your weight from the weight of you plus the bale to get the hay's weight. Then crack open a couple of bales and weigh yourself holding some representative flakes. Find an average of the weights, and you'll have a much better idea how much hay you're really feeding your horse when you toss him three flakes in the evening.

Weighing grain is most easily done with an ordinary kitchen scale. (Be sure to subtract the weight of the empty container you use to scoop your grain.) Remember that some grains are far more energy-dense than others, so any time you substitute one type of grain for another, you should repeat the weighing process to make sure that you're delivering an equivalent *weight*, not an equivalent *volume*. A one-quart scoop of corn will have considerably more energy than a one-quart scoop of oats — so if you feed that quart to a horse who is used to oats, you could have one excitable horse on your hands! (Keep in mind that it takes many days for a horse to adjust to changes in the energy content of his diet — so if you change feeds, do so gradually.)

We know from our chapter on fiber that under almost all circumstances, a horse's diet should consist of *at least 50%* forage. (The only exceptions are weanlings and yearlings, for whom grain might make up 70% and 60%, respectively, of their total diet as a maximum; and 2-year-olds in intense race training, who might receive up to 65% grain if necessary.) So of the 1.5% to 3.0% total feed an adult horse consumes daily, he should receive a *minimum* of 0.75% pasture, hay, or other fiber sources. He could, of course, receive up to 3.0% pasture or hay, if he is an easy keeper and/or idle or in light work. Going back to our 950-pound Morgan gelding, if we assume he, like most Morgans, is easy to keep weight on, and if we know he is used for pleasure riding only, he could survive quite nicely on 14.25 pounds of forage per day. If, on the other hand, he is very fit and is competing at the highest levels of combined driving, he might need a diet consisting of 14.25 pounds of hay, and another 14.25 pounds of grain daily to fuel his performance (for a total of 28.5 pounds of feed, or 3% of his bodyweight). When you do these figures, remember there's some room for adjustment — and that you also can factor in a 10% to 15% wastage factor for hay.

If you have good quality pasture and/or hay and are feeding a well-formulated commercial grain mix, you might never need to do more ration balancing than the above. To make sure your horse is getting enough protein, calcium, and phosphorus, use the chart on page 143 — and compare the requirements to the total amount in the diet you're providing. For example, if you are feeding your breeding stallion a legume hay with 15% crude protein (a figure you'll know from having run a hay analysis), and it makes up 50% of his ration, choose a low-protein grain (under 10%) to balance that high-protein hay. If, on the other hand, you are feeding a grass hay with only 8% crude protein, you can afford to offer a higher-protein grain ration. Under most circumstances, of course, it's very difficult to create a protein deficiency in an adult horse; but with a young, growing horse, or a mare who is nursing or in the last stage of pregnancy, protein, calcium, and phosphorus values are more crucial. Selecting a grain mix which is designed for the stage of life your horse is in is the easiest approach here — it can save you a lot of trouble (not to mention your calculator batteries).

## SPECIAL CASES

HIGH PERFORMANCE: the more work a horse does, the higher his energy requirement. While it's possible to calculate the exact digestible energy delivered by your horse's diet, for the average horse-owner, listening to your horse is enough. If

High performance = high energy requirements.

he is becoming fatigued earlier than you'd like as his workload is intensified, or if he's losing weight, it's time to supply more energy to the diet. That means increasing the amount of carbohydrates and fats he receives (which might necessitate reducing the amount of hay or forage he eats if you're nearing the 3% limit). If you have a high-performance horse who's already close to receiving the maximum amount of grain he should eat on a daily basis, however, consider adding some supplemental fat, in the form of vegetable oil, to his diet. As we noted in the chapter on feeding fat, it takes some time to 'kick in,' but fat is an excellent energy source, supplying almost two and a half times the energy of carbohydrates. It can provide an energy boost without increasing the overall volume of feed by more than an ounce or two.

PREGNANCY AND LACTATION: During the first eight months of pregnancy, a mare's nutritional needs are not much different than they would normally be. In the last three months, however, when the fetus is developing most rapidly, it makes significant demands on her body. Most researchers recommend a 2% rise in the level of crude protein a mare receives in the ninth and tenth months (from 8% to 10%), as well as an 85% increase in the amount of calcium, and a 100% increase in the amount of phosphorus she ingests. Copper, zinc, manganese, and iron are important for good bone and muscle growth and maturation in the foal and are best supplied now, as they are only present in low concentrations in mare's milk. In the 11th month, a further increase in protein level, to 11%, is recommended. Energy requirements in the mare also increase by about 20% in the last trimester. Typically, rations need to be changed from an early-pregnancy diet of about 80-90% forage to a 70% forage/30% concentrates diet as foaling approaches.

Also, keep in mind that mares in late gestation usually are being fed hay that has been in storage longer than three months. This means some deterioration of the fat-soluble vitamins A, D, and E. A commercially prepared vitamin supplement for broodmares can be an excellent addition to the diet at this time. (Problems with retained placentas after birth are also linked to inadequate selenium, calcium, and vitamin E in the diet — another good reason to supplement before foaling.)

**Nursing mares need nutritional support.**

Lactation, to many people's surprise, is actually more stressful to the mare than her pregnancy. During the first three months of nursing her foal, she will need significant nutritional support, including a diet that has 13% crude protein, high digestible energy (this is also a good time for a high-fat diet), and calcium and phosphorus levels of at least 0.5% and 0.35%. She also will need more total calories while nursing, and should be fed between 2.5% and 3.0% of her bodyweight in total feed per day. After the third month, as her foal begins to eat more solid food and nurse less often, her milk production gradually decreases, as do her nutrient and energy requirements. By the time the foal is weaned, she should be back to "pre-pregnancy" status in terms of her diet, regardless of whether she is open or was re-bred. If pregnant, the cycle of extra nutritional support will recur when she reaches the ninth-month stage.

NURSING FOALS: Because they are growing so rapidly, young foals have the highest nutrient and energy requirements of any age of horse. Continuing good nutritional support of the mare will ensure that the foal receives good nutrition in his milk, and most researchers recommend the use of a creep feed for foals as well. Such a feed is usually manufactured with a protein level of 16% to 18%, and includes milk protein, which has an optimal amino acid profile including high levels of lysine. Look, as well, for a calcium level close to, or even exceeding 0.9%, and a phosphorus level of 0.6% or better (but never exceeding the calcium level). Copper levels of upwards of 50 ppm are also a good idea, particularly if you live in an area with copper-deficient soils; and zinc levels, which affect copper absorption, should also be high, in the 60 ppm range.

Foals should be introduced to creep feed at three to four weeks of age, and at first likely will consume only about 300 g (a little over half a pound). By three or four months of age, though, they'll be eating over a kilogram a day, and be at three to four kilograms by the time they're weaned. Yeast culture, an inexpensive feed supplement which improves phosphorus utilization and the overall digestibility of grains, and also provides extra B vitamins, is a good idea for weanlings, as is a good-quality legume forage such as alfalfa hay.

(One important note: Though there is still much that researchers don't understand about developmental orthopedic disease (DOD), the catch-all term for a number of different bone and joint abnormalities that might develop in a horse's first year, it's now known that high levels of protein are not to blame — so restricting the protein level or caloric intake of a young horse is not only false economy, but may limit his optimum growth. It's suspected that DOD has more to do with certain mineral levels, environmental factors, and genetic predisposition.)

BREEDING STALLIONS: Many researchers feel that a stallion being used for breeding benefits from some supplemental protein (to 10%) and slightly elevated calcium and phosphorus levels. Breeding seems to be harder on some stallions than others, with some becoming quite ribby over the course of the breeding season; others positively thrive on the routine and need their grain cut back a little. Once the breeding season is over, a stallion should be maintained like any other adult horse, according to his work level.

THE 'HOT' HORSE: Many owners complain that their horses are too 'hot', or high-strung, to work with easily, and diet often gets the blame. The type of horse which tends to be hot is also the type which tends to be difficult to keep weight on (often a Thoroughbred or Thoroughbred-cross). This is something of a Catch-22 — if you reduce the feed, the horse is more manageable, but loses weight; increase the feed, and the horse maintains his weight but is wired for sound! Take heart; there are solutions.

Being 'hot' is often at least partly a function of temperament, but feeding more energy than the horse can find a constructive outlet for doesn't help. To find a healthier compromise, provide the hot horse with as much exercise as possible (that includes both work and turn-out time), and adjust his diet so that he receives enough total feed to keep his ribs covered, while delivering a more appropriate energy level. Reducing the amount of grain, and adding beet pulp to the grain ration, is one popular solution — in this way, you're supplementing the amount of low-energy, filling fiber your horse receives, but since it's mixed in with his grain, he hardly misses what he's not getting. Supplemental fat can also be useful here to help keep weight on, since any that is not used as an energy source is easily stored as fat (just as it does — far too easily — in our own bodies). The hot horse also benefits from generous quantities of forage. And if the horse still has too much energy for the work he does ... well, perhaps he's in the wrong line of work. He may be a square peg in a round hole as a Western pleasure horse, for example, but would find a happy home as an eventer or polo pony.

THE OVERWEIGHT HORSE: the answer is as simple, and difficult, as it is for humans. Eat less, and exercise! Certain types of horses seem to be 'air ferns' — they can survive, and become quite plump, on a diet that seems to provide far too little for the average horse. Some pony breeds, in particular, have to be managed very carefully, because they are at greater risk of laminitis if they consume large amounts of grain, or even graze on sweet spring grass. As cruel as it might sound, it can be healthier to keep such a horse or pony on a 'dry lot' rather than a pasture with good grazing — at least until the rich new growth has stopped in the heat of the summer. Careful monitoring of the amount of forage consumed should be coupled with lots of exercise. And unless the horse is in intense work, he can probably get by with no grain at all. In order to ensure that he is receiving a correct complement of vitamins and minerals, look for a supplement which is designed to balance a high-forage diet; many feed companies have such supplements available.

THE OLDER HORSE: Advances in medical treatment as well as nutrition mean that we have more geriatric horses with us than ever before. This is not necessarily a bad thing; many horses in their 20s and 30s continue to be productive individuals whose wisdom and patience make them a joy to have around. But as a horse ages, his nutritional needs change, and we cannot merely assume that what worked in the past will work in the future. Older horses tend to have dental problems; often, the grinding surfaces have worn down so much that he loses much of his ability to chew fibrous matter like hay. This can be a primary cause of an older horse's inability to maintain good condition. In addition, the internal organs become less efficient at digesting nutrients — particularly, protein, phosphorus, and fiber. Because of this, it's worth seeking out a feed which offers slightly higher levels of these nutrients, and is relatively soft and easy to chew; a number of feed companies now offer formulas specifically designed for geriatrics, though any pelleted ration will likely be a better choice than unprocessed whole grains.

Choosing a soft, leafy hay with a higher concentration of legumes is also a good idea, as your older horse may have trouble chewing and digesting a stemmy, fibrous grass hay. And if your horse has trouble maintaining his weight, particularly in the winter months, the addition of some vegetable oil to the diet (up to two cups a day, depending on his size) can provide him with more energy and calories

Extremely aged horses, with no teeth to speak of, can sometimes be maintained quite comfortably by soaking forage and grain to make a "mush." Hay cubes, soaked in warm water for an hour or so before feeding, become quite manageable, and beet pulp can help provide more fiber; pelleted grains can also be soaked to make them much easier to chew.

Regular veterinary maintenance is also a good idea for an older horse. He may need his teeth floated on a quarterly instead of twice-yearly basis, and it's useful to run a blood profile periodically as well, to pick up "red flags" such as impaired liver or kidney function. (Horses with renal or liver failure cannot tolerate high levels of protein and may need other dietary adjustments as well.)

## AND FINALLY, A FEW MISCELLANEOUS TIPS:

• When switching from one form of feed to another, do it gradually over a number of days or even weeks. Horses adapt to changes in hay more quickly than they do changes in grain. If you switch from one form of grain to another (for example, if you change from a sweet feed to an extruded ration), expect your horse to take a few days to get used to the difference in format. Start with a small amount, and work back up to his usual level.

• Reduce grain by half if your horse is not working — for instance, if an injury forces him to be maintained on stall rest, or on a rest day if he is in steady work.

• Remember to feed by weight, not by volume. If you switch from a legume hay to a grass hay, weigh the bales so that you are able to feed an equivalent amount. Likewise, if you switch from oats to a pelleted ration — or even if you switch from one sweet feed brand to another — weigh the amount of the old ration your horse was eating, and then weigh the new ration to find what a comparable volume will be. They will not necessarily be the same level in the coffee can.

• While some horses are just picky eaters, on the whole, a healthy horse usually has a healthy appetite. To tempt a fussy horse, you might have to experiment a bit to discover what he finds most palatable. If your horse consistently leaves some hay and/or grain after he has exercised strenuously, reduce the fiber and bulk in his ration by about 10%. If he still doesn't clean up what he is given, consider that pain induced by his work may be leaving him with no appetite. Try scaling back his workouts to see if that remedies the problem; a veterinary exam also might be in order.

• If a horse cleans up his feed and still appears hungry, first increase the amount of hay or forage he receives by about 10%. Only increase the amount of grain if the horse appears lethargic or is under an increasing workload.

• Ask your local agriculture extension specialist about the levels of selenium in your local soil. Be careful only to use selenium-supplemented feeds if you live in a selenium-deficient area, and never combine a selenium-supplemented feed with another top-dressed supplement containing selenium. The toxicity level of this mineral is unusually low.

• Provide fresh water at all times (except immediately after hard exercise, when ingesting large amounts of cold water can cause a horse to colic). It's worth testing your water periodically to ensure it is safe and has no toxic levels of heavy metals or bacteria, particularly if you draw your water from a well.

• Soaking your hay can reduce dust levels significantly. If you have no choice but to feed a dusty hay, or if you have a horse with respiratory problems (such as chronic obstructive pulmonary disease, also called 'heaves' or 'broken wind'), wet each flake down thoroughly before you feed it.

• All grains have an inverted calcium:phosphorus ratio — that is, they contain more phosphorus than calcium. Balanced with hay, which has more calcium than phosphorus (especially in the case of legumes), your horse's overall diet usually will end up with a healthy calcium:phosphorus ratio of 1:1, or slightly higher. It's important for the growth and maintenance of good bones, tendons, and ligaments that there is at least as much calcium as phosphorus in the diet; the ideal ratio is 1.2:1 to 1.6:1, but horses can actually tolerate diets with as much as six times calcium as phosphorus without any visible side-effects. If you feed a ration that is heavy on the concentrates and light on hay and forages, you may need to supplement calcium to achieve a better balance.

• Wheat bran has an extremely inverted calcium:phosphorus ratio — 0.1% calcium to 1.3%, or a 1:13 ratio. As a result, it should never be fed in large quantities on a daily basis, as it is likely to trigger "bran disease" (sometimes called "big head"), a condition in which the horse's system leaches calcium from the bones in order to try to balance the high concentration of phosphorus being taken in. (The result is porous, brittle bones, and it can be irreversible.) Furthermore, bran has been shown not to have the laxative effect many people credit it with — the loose manure that results after a bran mash is actually the result of a mild digestive upset from a sudden change in feed. A once-a-week bran mash on a cold winter's night, or to tempt the appetite of a convalescing horse, does no harm, but bran should never be fed to young, growing horses, and in an adult horse's diet it should make up no more than 10% of the total grain ration.

• Have your hay analyzed each time you get a new batch in. Don't assume that bales from the same grower will have the same nutrition from year to year, or even from first cut to second.

• Commercial sweet feeds and pelleted rations may come in two varieties: 'least-cost' formulations and 'fixed' formulations. In a least-cost formulation, ingredients may be substituted periodically according to the fluctuations of the grain market, in order to keep the price at a constant level. As a result, the nutrition a least-cost formulation delivers may vary quite a bit. A fixed formula, on the other hand, relies on a single recipe that does not change, so its price may fluctuate according to the price of its ingredients. From the point of view of reliable nutrition, a fixed formula feed, while somewhat more expensive, is the better bet.

• When you buy a commercially balanced grain ration and couple it with an appropriate, good-quality hay, extra top-dressing with vitamin/mineral supplements is not only unnecessary, but could unbalance the nutrition of the ration. At worst, it might even deliver dangerous quantities of some nutrients; at best, it's a waste of money. Resist the temptation to tinker with what the company's nutritionists have taken so much care to formulate!

• Feed small amounts, often. Horses who are fed three or even four small grain meals a day have significantly lower incidence of colic and other health problems than those who only get one or two large meals a day.

• No horse will get good value from his feed if his teeth have sharp points or hooks, or if intestinal parasites are battling him for the nutrients he ingests. Have your horse's teeth floated twice-yearly (or more often if he needs it), and de-worm him regularly with a drug such as ivermectin or moxidectin, which kills a wide variety of parasites, including bots.

## A FINAL THOUGHT

A well-known equine nutrition and exercise physiology researcher recently remarked to me that, of all the facets of horse management, she thought nutrition was the most poorly understood and most widely mis-managed area of all. If you've gotten this far, congratulations. You're now equipped to go out there and make a difference in how your horses are fed — and to do it from a base of knowledge and common sense.

### Major Nutrient Requirements of Horse

| Class of Horse | Crude Protein % | Digestible Energy (DE) in Mcal/kg | Calcium % | Phosphorus % | Expected Total Feed Eaten(% bodyweight /day) |
|---|---|---|---|---|---|
| Nursing foal 2-4 months, (needs above milk) | 16 | 3.3 - 3.8 | 0.9 | 0.6 | 0.5 - 0.75 |
| Weanling at 4 months | 14.5 | 2.9 | 0.8 | 0.5 | 2.5 - 3.5 |
| Weanling at 6 months | 14.5 | 2.9 | 0.7 | 0.4 | 2.5 - 3.5 |
| Yearling (12 months) | 12.5 | 2.8 | 0.5 | 0.3 | 2.0 - 3.0 |
| Long yearling (18 months) | 12 | 2.65 | 0.4 | 0.25 | 2.0 - 2.75 |
| Two-year-old (24 months) | 11 | 2.5 | 0.35 | 0.2 | 2.0 - 2.5 |
| Mature horse — maintenance (idle) | 8 | 2.0 | 0.25 | 0.2 | 1.5 - 2.0 |
| Mature horse in light work (eg. pleasure riding) | 10 | 2.45 | 0.3 | 0.25 | 1.5 - 2.5 |
| Mature horse in moderate work (eg. jumping, cutting, ranch work) | 10.5 | 2.65 | 0.3 | 0.25 | 1.75 - 2.5 |
| Mature horse in intense work (eg. polo, racing, endurance) | 11.5 | 2.85 | 0.35 | 0.25 | 2.0 - 3.0 |
| Stallion in breeding season | 10 | 2.4 | 0.3 | 0.25 | 1.5 - 2.5 |
| Pregnant mare — first nine months | 8 | 2.0 | 0.25 | 0.2 | 1.5 - 2.0 |
| Pregnant mare — 9th and 10th months | 10 | 2.25 | 0.5 | 0.35 | 1.5 - 2.0 |
| Pregnant mare — 11th month | 11 | 2.4 | 0.5 | 0.35 | 1.5 - 2.0 |
| Nursing mare — first three months | 13 | 2.6 | 0.5 | 0.35 | 2.5 - 3.0 |
| Nursing mare — from third month on | 11 | 2.45 | 0.35 | 0.25 | 2.0 - 2.5 |

# Body Condition Scoring System

| Condition score | General Condition | Description |
| --- | --- | --- |
| 1 | Very poor | Animal extremely emaciated; no fatty tissues can be felt. Spine bones easily visible, ends feel pointed; tailhead and hip bones prominent, ribs visible and skin furrows between them. |
| 2 | Very thin | Animal emaciated, very minimal fat covering. Spine visible but ends feel rounded; tailhead and hip bones obvious. Ribs prominent with slight depressions between them. |
| 3 | Thin | Fat buildup halfway on vertical spines, but easily discernible; flat spinal bones not felt.Tailhead prominent, hip bones appear rounded, but visible. Slight flat cover over ribs, but rib outline obvious. Withers prominent but with some fat cover. |
| 4 | Moderately thin | Withers not obviously thin; neck carries some fat. Slight ridge along back. Fat felt on tailhead. Faint outline of ribs. |
| 5 | Moderate | Neck blends smoothly into body; withers rounded over top. Back is level - spine neither protrudes nor is "buried." Fat around tailhead begins to feel spongy. Ribs not seen but easily felt. |
| 6 | Moderately fleshy | Back may have slight inward crease. Fat around tailhead feels soft, as does fat over ribs. Fat layer visible over shoulder. |
| 7 | Fleshy | Visible fat deposits on neck and behind shoulder. Firm fat covering over withers. Slight inward crease down back. Individual ribs can still be felt. |
| 8 | Fat | Noticeable thickening of neck; area behind shoulder filled in flush with the body. Crease down back quite evident. Tailhead fat, very soft, and flabby. Difficult to feel ribs. |
| 9 | Extremely fat | Bulging fat on neck, shoulder, and withers. Obvious deep crease down back. Patchy fat over ribs. Fat along inner hind legs may rub together. Flank filled with flush. |

(adapted from Henneke et al (1983), *Equine Vet Journal* 371-372)

## Amount of Feed Recommended for Growing Horses

| Horse | Age (months) | Grain mix (% of Total Diet) | Kg of Grain mix per 100 bodyweight /day | Kg grain mix/day/ month of age for ponies ** | Kg grain mix/day/ month of age for horses |
|---|---|---|---|---|---|
| Nursing foals | 0 - 4 | 100 | 0.5 - 0.75 | 0.1 | 0.45 |
| Weanlings | 4 - 12 | 70 | 1.7 - 2.0 | 0.25 | 0.7 |
| Yearlings | 12 - 18 | 60 | 1.3 - 1.7 | * | * |
| Long yearlings | 8 - 24 | 50 | 1.0 - 1.25 | * | * |
| Two-year-olds | 24 - 36 | 50 | 1.0 - 1.25 | * | * |

* For all ages of horses, feed grain only up to a maximum of 0.9 kg/100 kg of anticipated mature weight per day.
** Ponies: anticipated mature weight of 225 kg (500 lbs) or less.

## Horses' Major Nutrient Needs in Diet Dry Matter as Compared to the Content of Common Feeds

| | Digestible Energy Mcal/kg | Protein (%) | Calcium (%) | Phosphorus (%) |
|---|---|---|---|---|
| **Needed for:** Maintenance | 2.0 | 8 | 0.25 | 0.20 |
| Working horses and breeding stallions | 2.5 - 2.9 | 10 - 11 | 0.3 | 0.25 |
| Aged horses | 2.2 | 10 | 0.25 | 0.25 |
| **Composition of:** Legumes | 2.2 - 2.4 | 15 - 20 | 0.8 - 2.0 | 0.15 - 0.3 |
| Grasses, mature | 1.5 - 2.2 | 6 - 10 | 0.3 - 0.5 | 0.15 - 0.3 |
| Cereal grains | 3.3 - 3.7 | 9 - 12 | 0.02 - 0.1 | 0.25 - 0.35 |

# GLOSSARY

**Acid Detergent Fiber** — A value used to describe a feed's fiber content, ADF is a measure of the cellulose and lignin content of a feed. It is the most accurate description available of a feed's fiber digestibility level, but because it removes hemicellulose from consideration as well as starches, it underestimates a feed's insoluble fiber content and overestimates its energy content and feeding value.

**Aerobic** — Occurring in the presence of air. In terms of exercising horses, aerobic metabolism is that which is fueled by oxygen. Opposite of anaerobic, meaning without oxygen.

**Amino Acids** — Simple organic compounds, made up of a basic amino group (COOH) and an acidic carboxyl group. The "building blocks" for the growth and repair of the horse's bones, muscles, and other structures. There are 22 different amino acids, each containing nitrogen and sometimes sulfur. "Essential amino acids" are those the horse cannot synthesize himself and must take in from his feed (8 to 10 of the 22). The rest are "non-essential amino acids," which can be manufactured out of other molecules within the horse's system.

**Amylase** — A digestive enzyme, secreted by the pancreas, which is instrumental in breaking the alpha bonds of carbohydrates to create smaller disaccharide molecules of maltose.

**Anaerobic threshold** — The point at which the horse can no longer function by aerobic metabolism, occurring at a heartrate of 140 to 150 beats per minute.

**Anemia** — Below normal count of red blood cells in the blood. Nutritional causes in horses may include excess zinc or selenium, and either a dietary surplus or deficiency of vitamin A. Increased intake of iron, protein, and B vitamins may be helpful in correcting the condition.

**Anti-oxidant** — A substance which prevents tissues or objects from being oxidized (combining with oxygen). In the body, oxidation can be destructive to cells. Common nutritional anti-oxidants are vitamins C and E, citric acid, butylated hydroxyanisole (BHA), and butylate hydroxytoluene (BHT).

**Ascorbate or Ascorbic Acid** — Vitamin C.

**ATP (adenosine triphosphate)** — The only source of energy which can be used by muscles and other body tissues. Energy from carbohydrates, fats, or proteins is converted into ATP to allow transfer to the body tissues for uses such as muscle contraction or brain function.

**Balanced diet** — A diet which provides the proper amounts and proportions of all required nutrients.

**Beta-carotene** — A yellow plant pigment, some of which is converted in the intestinal wall to vitamin A.

**Biotin** — A B vitamin, thought to be important for the growth of healthy hooves.

**Blister beetles** — Poisonous beetles which can inhabit bales of alfalfa hay. Cantharidin, the toxic substance in the beetles, produces inflammation and blisters within a few hours of exposure; if the toxin is ingested, it can cause severe poisoning or even death. As cantharidin is quite stable and just as poisonous in dead beetles as live ones, extended storage of affected hay bales will not decrease their toxicity. Symptoms of blister beetle poisoning include acute colic symptoms, "playing" in water without drinking, and frequent urination.

**Boot stage** — The stage at which seed heads first appear in a hay crop.

**Bots** — The larvae of the bot fly, which attach to the interior lining of the stomach and may cause colic, inflammation, and perforation of the stomach wall.

**Bran** — The outer layer of the grain kernel, removed in the process of milling.

**Bran disease** — Enlargement skull bones, due to replacement of calcium with fibrous connective tissue. Jaw and face bones are most obviously affected, though the condition affects bones throughout the body. Caused by a dietary phosphorus excess or calcium deficiency, which can result from feeding large quantities of wheat bran. Also called "big head disease."

**Calcium:phosphorus ratio** — The amount of calcium with respect to the amount of phosphorus in the diet.

**Calorie** — If spelled with a small "c," the amount of energy needed to raise the temperature of one gram of water one degree Celsius (sometimes called "standard calorie"); if spelled with a capital "C," the amount of energy needed to raise the temperature of one kilogram of water one degree (also called kilocalorie). One kilocalorie = 1,000 standard calories. Kilocalories are the smallest unit used in nutritional research.

**Carbohydrates** — Compounds made up of carbon, hydrogen, and oxygen whose major nutritional function is to provide energy to the horse. Starches, sugars, and cellulose and hemi-cellulose are some of the more important carbohydrates.

**Cecum** — Part of the horse's large intestine, the site of the "fermentation vat" where plant fibers are broken down by beneficial gut bacteria. The physiological equivalent of the human appendix, but far more useful and less troublesome.

**Cellulose** — A carbohydrate which forms the "skeleton" of most plants. Animals do not produce the enzymes to digest it, but their gut microflora do.

**Chaff** — Seed hulls, chopped straw, or low-quality hay, added to feed to make a horse eat more slowly. High in fiber and low in energy.

**Chelation** — A process by which a mineral is bound to an organic molecule such as a carbohydrate or protein. If the organic molecule is more readily absorbed in the intestine than the mineral, chelation increases the amount of the mineral absorbed.

**Chlorophyll** — The green pigment of a plant.

**Chronic obstructive pulmonary disease (COPD)** — Also called heaves or broken wind. A chronic respiratory condition causing shortened breath, labored breathing, coughing, and decreased exercise tolerance. Often triggered by an allergy.

**Cobalamine** — Vitamin B12.

**Colic** — A catch-all term describing abdominal pain in the horse. Nutritional causes can include inadequate fiber intake, excess grain, or a sudden change in feed. Ingestion of blister beetles in alfalfa hay also can trigger colic.

**Colon** — A portion of the large intestine which extends from the cecum to the rectum.

**Complete feed** — A feed which contains all of the nutrients needed by the horse, with the exception of water and salt. Generally used to describe a commercially prepared ration which contains both forage and grain.

**Concentrates** — A broad description of high-energy, low-fiber (under 18%) feeds. Most often used to describe grains, but considered to include anything that is not a forage or roughage product.

**Crimped** — Grain which is pressed between corrugated rollers to crack the kernels, thus increasing its digestibility.

**Crude Fiber** — An estimate of the total amount of fiber in a feed. It overestimates the non-fiber, carbohydrate content of a feed, and underestimates the cellulose portion, which leads to an overall overestimation of the feed's caloric content and feeding value. Nonetheless, the crude fiber value is the one most often listed on feed tags.

**Crude Protein (CP)** — A value based on the overall nitrogen content of a feed. To arrive at a CP value, divide the nitrogen content of the feed by 0.16.

**Dehydrating** — Removing all of the moisture from a feed so as to prevent it from spoiling during storage.

**Developmental Orthopedic Disease (DOD)** — A blanket term for abnormalities in the growth and development of bones and joints in young horses. Some cases of DOD may be triggered, in part, by incorrect nutrition.

**Diarrhea** — Loose feces, caused by an above-normal amount of moisture. Nutritional causes include inadequate fiber, excess grain, a sudden change in diet, or a deficiency or excess of selenium.

**Digestible energy (DE)** — A value used to describe the amount of energy contained in a feed which can be used by the horse. Usually expressed in Mcal.

**Dry lot** — A fenced area with no grazing.

**Dry matter** — The portion of a feed which is not moisture. A feed which is 10% moisture is described as 90% dry matter. When feed comparisons are made, be careful not to directly compare "as fed" values with dry matter values, for they will be significantly different.

**Early bloom** — The period from which plants first begin to bloom, until one-tenth are in blossom. Used to describe the growth stage of hay fields.

**Easy keeper** — An animal which requires less feed than others to maintain good condition. The opposite type of horse is called a "hard keeper."

**Electrolytes** — In horses, this term is used to describe minerals lost in sweat and urine, primarily sodium, potassium, and chloride.

**Ergot** — A fungus (*Claviceps species*) which grows on the seeds of cereal grains such as rye, wheat, and oats, and grasses such as Kentucky bluegrass. It is poisonous if ingested and causes constriction of the arteries and decreasing blood flow to tissues, even causing gangrene in the extremities in sever cases. Ergot also can trigger abortion and nervous system disorders.

**Extrusion** — The process of forcing a feed through small openings under high pressure. The sudden release of pressure causes the feed to expand like popping corn.

**Fats** — Fats and oils are triglycerides, composed of glycerol (a long chain of carbon atoms) attached to a fatty acid. Fats are necessary in the horse's diet for the absorption of fat-soluble vitamins such as vitamin K, A, D, and E, and as a source of fatty acids needed for body structure. Fats are also a good source of energy, providing more than 2.25 times as much energy than a similar weight of carbohydrates or protein. Fats can be derived from plant and animal sources.

**Fat soluble vitamins** — Vitamins A, D, E, and K, which are absorbed in the small intestine and can be reserved in the fatty tissues.

**Fatty Acids** — See volatile fatty acids (VFA).

**Fiber** — A carbohydrate composed of simple sugars bound by "beta bonds," which must be broken in the intestinal tract by gut microflora in order for the horse to utilize the energy contained in the feed. Fiber is composed of three main substances, cellulose, hemicellulose, and lignin, and of soluble fiber. See also soluble fiber.

**Fixed formulation** — A commercial grain mix which has a set recipe. The price of such a feed may fluctuate according to the grain market, but the nutrition it delivers will remain the same. See also "least-cost formulation."

**Floating the teeth** — Filing down the sharp points of enamel on the teeth that develop when horses consume a domestic diet. Generally performed by a veterinarian with a file or rasp, at least once a year.

**Forage** — Plant material, usually grasses (fresh or dried) that make up the basis of the equine diet. Forage may be any feed which contains more than 18% crude fiber.

**Founder** — See laminitis.

**Free-choice** — Feed or water made available to the horse so that he can consume as much as he chooses.

**Gastrointestinal tract** — The internal organs responsible for the breakdown and digestion of food. Includes the mouth, tongue, eosophagus, stomach, small intestine, cecum, large intestine, rectum, and anus.

**Glucagon** — A hormone which converts stored glycogen back into glucose and releasing it into the bloodstream.

**Glucose** — A simple sugar or monosaccharide that is metabolized by animals for energy.

**Glycogen** — A storage form of glucose, present primarily in the muscles and liver.

**Glycolysis** — The utilization of glucose and glycogen.

**Grain** — The seeds of plants used for food, eg. corn, oats, barley, wheat, and rice.

**Groats** — Cereal grain kernels after the hulls have been removed; usually used to describe hull-less oats.

**Haylage** — Hay or grass which is cut and placed in plastic to ferment before it dries. Highly nutritious but vulnerable to mold and bacterial growth if the packaging is punctured. Also called "horsehage."

**Heartgirth** — The circumference of the horse around the barrel, just behind the front legs (roughly where the heart is located). Measured to help calculate a horse's weight.

**Heaves** — See Chronic Obstructive Pulmonary Disease.

**Hemicellulose** — A polysaccharide molecule which, along with cellulose, makes up the insoluble fiber of a plant. Hemicellulose is found in the non-seed and non-fruit portions of the plant (the leaves, stems, and hulls).

**Hindgut** — The large intestine, including the cecum, ascending colon, small colon, rectum, and anus.

**Hulls** — Outer protective covering of grains.

**Ileum** — The terminal section of the small intestine, leading to the hindgut.

**Insoluble fiber** — Hemicellulose plus cellulose, some of which is digestible by the horse with the help of fiber-digesting bacteria in the gut. The higher the insoluble fiber content of a feed, the lower the amount of usable dietary energy provided.

**Insulin** — A hormone which regulates the amount of glucose in the bloodstream.

**IU** — International Units, a measure used to describe quantities of vitamins in the diet.

**Kilocalorie** — See calorie.

**Lactase** — A digestive enzyme, produced in the cells of the small intestine, which helps break down lactose (milk sugar) into its component monosaccharides. Present only in young horses.

**Lactation** — Producing milk.

**Lactic acid** — Produced as a byproduct when glucose or glycogen are used for energy in the absence of oxygen. Once produced in the exercising muscle, it must be removed and transported back to the liver or kidney for utilization. If production exceeds the removal rate, it accumulates in the muscle, causing fatigue and pain and inhibiting further energy production. If present minus its hydrogen ion, it is called lactate.

**Lactose** — Milk sugar, a disaccharide consisting of one molecule of glucose bonded to one molecule of galactose. Present in mare's milk.

**Laminitis** — An inflammation of the laminae of the horse's foot, causing pressure, pain, and tissue damage, and resulting in separation of the hoof wall from the laminae. Laminitis can be caused by consuming large amounts of cold water immediately after strenuous exercise, consuming excessively large amounts of grain or lush green spring grass (grass founder, especially common in ponies), infectious disease such as enteritis, pneumonia, or uterine infections following foaling, severe concussion to the feet from running on hard surfaces (road founder).

**Late bloom** — The period when the majority of blossoms begin to dry and fall off the plant. Used in regard to hay fields. A field in late bloom is past its best nutritional value.

**Least-cost formulation** — A commercial grain ration which has a set price, and might substitute certain ingredients, such as protein supplements, when the price of one increases. The nutrition such a feed delivers will be similar, but not necessarily exactly the same from batch to batch.

**Legumes** — Plants which obtain nitrogen through bacteria that live in their root nodules. Includes alfalfa, clovers, birdsfoot trefoil, and peas.

**Lignasol** — A binder which is used to help hold grain particles together in the pelleting process.

**Lignin** — A major component of the cell wall of some high-fiber plants, lignin contributes to a plant's rigidity. Also one of the three main components of dietary fiber, considered indigestible to the horse.

**Linseed** — Also called flax seed. A source of oils and protein. Linseed cake or meal is often used as a protein supplement, although its amino acid profile is poor. Flax seeds may also be boiled to make a linseed jelly, reputed to add a bloom on the coat and help a thin horse put on weight. However, linseed should not be fed raw, as it contains cyanogenetic glycosides which, when exposed to damage from drought, frost, or wilting of the flax plant, may release cyanide. Heat processing destroys the enzymes which release the cyanide, making linseed safe to feed.

**Lipids** — See fats.

**Lucerne** — Alfalfa.

**Lysine** — The "first limiting" amino acid, important for growth in young horses. If sufficient lysine is not present in the horse's system, he will be unable to fully utilize all the other amino acids available. The amount of lysine in the diet is less crucial for adult horses than for young growing ones.

**Macrominerals** — Minerals needed in relatively large quantities in the diet.

**Maintenance diet** — A diet adequate to maintain a horse's condition when he is at rest in a climate where the temperature does not require additional energy to heat or cool the body.

**Maltase** — A digestive enzyme which breaks down maltose to its monosaccharide components.

**Mcal** — Megacalorie, the usual unit used in equine nutrition. Equal to 1,000 kilocalories. See also calorie.

**Metabolism** — Chemical reactions in the body, including the utilization of nutrients following their absorption from the intestine.

**Microflora** — A normal, beneficial population of bacteria. In the horse's digestive system, gut microflora assist in digestion.

**Microminerals** — Minerals needed in minute quantities in the horse's diet.

**Micronizing** — A cooking process for commercial grain feeds, said to improve starch digestibility.

**Minerals** — Inorganic (non-carbon-containing) elements required in the diet to facilitate many metabolic functions.

**Mycotoxins** — Harmful substances produced by molds and fungi, growing on feeds particularly in warm, moist conditions.

**Neutral Detergent Fiber (NDF)** — A value used to describe a feed's fiber content. It includes almost all of the cellulose in a feed sample, and over 50% of the hemicellulose, but also includes an overestimation of the feed's digestible starch level.

**Niacin** — A B vitamin which has no numerical designation.

**Nutrient** — Any feed ingredient necessary for the support of life. Includes carbohydrates, fats, proteins, minerals, fiber, vitamins, and water.

**Nuts** — In the United Kingdom, feed pellets or cubes may be known as "pony nuts" or simply, "nuts."

**Omnivorous** — An animal whose diet includes both plant and animal material is said to be omnivorous. Humans are omnivorous, while horses are strict herbivores (plant-eaters).

**Organic molecule** — Any molecule which contains carbon.

**Oxidation** — Combining with oxygen. In the field of nutrition, this may mean a feed has been stored too long and has oxidized, losing some of its nutritional value. Oxidation may also mean "burning," as when a sample of feed is burned in a lab to determine its caloric value.

**Palatability** — The desirability of a feed (how much a horse wishes to consume it).

**Pantothenic acid** — A B vitamin, formerly designated B3.

**Pellets** — Grains that are ground, bound together, and pushed through small holes at low pressure to make cylindrical shapes.

**pH** — A measurement of acidity or alkalinity, ranging from 0 to 14. A pH level of 7 is neutrality, below that is acidic (has a high hydrogen ion concentration), and above 7 is alkaline or basic (has a low hydrogen ion activity).

**Polysaccharides** — See saccharides.

**Preservatives** — Substances added to feed to decrease the rate of decomposition of the nutrients within. Preservatives enhance a feed's stability and resistance to spoilage, discoloration, oxidation, mold, and bacterial growth.

**Protein** — Chains of amino acids, which are broken up into their components during the digestive process and used for the growth and repair of tissues. The position and number of amino acids in a single protein make up its "amino acid profile."

**Protein supplements** — High protein ingredients used to supplement the protein content of a mixed grain ration. Common plant sources of protein include soybean meal, cottonseed meal, and linseed meal. Of these, soybean meal has the best amino acid profile and lysine content, so is better utilized than cottonseed or linseed meal. Protein can also be derived from animal sources such as feather or bone meal, and from milk (the preferred source for foal rations).

**Pyroxidine** — Vitamin B6.

**Rectum** — The terminal end of the large intestine, leading from the colon to the anus.

**Renal** — Referring to the kidneys.

**Retinol** — Vitamin A.

**Reverse peristalsis** — A muscle contraction reflex that sends food back up to the mouth from the stomach. Horses lack this reflex.

**Riboflavin** — Vitamin B2.

**Rice bran** — The outer covering of rice grains, sometimes used as a high-fat feed supplement.

**Roughage** — A non-forage feed which is high in fiber (over 18% crude fiber) and low in digestible energy. Beet pulp, straw, corn cobs, and cereal grain hulls are common roughage feeds for horses.

**Saccharides** — Soluble carbohydrates, such as starch, sugars, and glycogen. The prefixes mono-, di-, tri-, and poly- describe the number of the sugar molecules which are bonded together in the substance. For example, sucrose is a disaccharide composed of one molecule of glucose and one of fructose. Starch and glycogen are polysaccharides.

**Silage** — Fermented forage plants. The process is sometimes described as "ensiling." Haylage is produced by ensiling chopped hay in plastic.

**Simple Sugars** — Also called monosaccharides. Fructose, glucose, galactose, and xylose are examples of simple sugars which, when bound together by alpha bonds, make up polysaccharide carbohydrate molecules.

**Soluble Fiber** — Highly digestible fiber from the liquid portions of a plant (the resin, sap, pectins, and mucilages).

**Solubles** — Liquids containing dissolved substances obtained from processing animal or plant materials.

**Starch** — A carbohydrate composed of many glucose molecules attached together with alpha bonds. The bonds are broken by digestive enzymes, releasing the glucose molecules so that they can be absorbed and used by the horse. Starch is the major source of dietary energy provided by grains.

**Straw** — The stems of cereal grains, after the removal of the grain or seeds. Used as bedding and also as a high-fiber, low energy "filler" feed.

**Sugar** — A soluble carbohydrate made up of monosaccharides.

**Supplement** — A feed additive used to increase the amount of a specific nutrient or nutrients in the diet.

**Sweet feed** — A grain mix containing molasses.

**Tallow** — Fat derived from animal sources, usually solid at room temperatures. Horses can digest tallow very well, but find it unpalatable.

**Textured ration** — Used by the feed industry to describe a grain mix, usually a sweet feed.

**Thiamin** — Vitamin B1.

**Total Digestible Nutrients (TDN)** — A term used to describe the energy density of a feed. Calculated by adding the percentage of digestible fat multiplied by 2.25, the digestible protein, and digestible carbohydrates and fiber present in the feed. One pound of TDN is equal to approximately 2,000 Kcalories of digestible energy.

**Toxin** — A poisonous substance.

**Trace mineral** — A mineral required only in very small amounts in the diet. Also called micromineral.

**Urea** — Produced in the liver and excreted primarily in the urine, urea is the body's major means of excreting excess nitrogen (produced by the breakdown of body or dietary protein). Composed of two molecules of ammonia attached to one molecule of carbon monoxide. While ruminants can digest and absorb urea, horses utilize very little of it.

**Vitamins** — Organic compounds needed in minute amounts for normal body functions. Vitamins supply no energy and are not a part of body structure, though some are produced in the horse's body. (Others must be sourced from the diet.)

**Volatile Fatty Acids (VFA)** — A chain of carbon atoms attached to a carboxylic acid (COOH), and the major source of dietary energy derived from forages and fiber. Fibrous plant products are broken down by fermentation in the gut until they are in the form of VFAs (including proprionic and butyric acids), which can be absorbed through the gut wall and stored for future energy use.

**Water-soluble vitamins** — The B vitamins and vitamin C, which are readily excreted by the horse and thus must be replaced on a regular basis. Some are manufactured by the horse's body itself, and others are sourced from the environment.

# INDEX

# RECOMMENDED READINGS

Ewing, R. A. *Beyond the Hay Days: A Refreshingly Simple Guide to Effective Horse Nutrition*. 1st ed. LaSalle, Colo.: PixyJack Press, 1997.

Lewis, L. D. *Equine Clinical Nutrition*. Baltimore: Williams & Wilkins, 1995.

Cuddeford, D. *Equine Nutrition*. Wiltshire, England: Crowood Press, 1996.

Frape, D. L. *Equine Nutrition and Feeding*. 2nd ed. Malden, Mass.: Blackwell Science, 1997.

Lewis, L. D. *Feeding and Care of the Horse*. 2nd ed. Baltimore: Williams & Wilkins, 1996.

Kohnke, J. *Feeding and Nutrition: The Making of a Champion*. Rouse Hill, NSW, Australia: Barubi Pacific, 1992.

Equine Research. *Feeding to Win*. Grand Prairie, Texas.: Equine Research Inc., 1992.

Northrup, A. A. *Feeds and Nutrient Management for the Horse: Back to Basics: A Common Sense Approach for the Weary Consumer*. Malta, Ill.: Communications Connections, 1997.

Cunha, T. J. *Horse Feeding and Nutrition*. 2nd ed. San Diego: Academic Press, 1991.

Hintz, H. F. *Horse Nutrition: A Practical Guide*. New York, N.Y.: Arco, 1983.

Pilliner, S. *Horse Nutrition and Feeding*. Boston: Blackwell Scientific Publications, 1992.

National Research Council (U.S.) Subcommittee on Horse Nutrition. *Nutrient Requirements of Horses*. 5th rev. ed. Washington, D.C.: National Academy Press, 1989.

# Equine Nutrition sites on the Internet

The Horse Interactive's nutrition section: http://www.thehorse.com/nutrition/

Feeding and Nutrition articles from The Mane Points, published by Southern States Cooperative: http://www2.sscoop.com/sscoop/mp/nutrition/nutrit.html

Feeding and Nutrition from the Equine Veterinary Network:http://www.equinevetnet.com/pages/nutritionmenu.html

Feeds and Feeding Horses and Equine Nutrition from The Horseman's Advisor: http://www.horscadvicc.com/articlcs/horsccarc/feedmenu.html

Horse Care articles (includes several nutrition-related articles) from Equijournal: http://www.equijournal.com/equijournal/horsecare.html

# Picture Credits

CHAPTER 2
Jamie Donaldson, 20.

CHAPTER 3
CLiX Photography, 27, 30; Anne M. Eberhardt, 28.

CHAPTER 4
Barbara D. Livingston, 35; Anne M. Eberhardt, 38, 41; Brant Gamma, 39.

CHAPTER 5
Harold Campton, 47; Anne M. Eberhardt, 49, 51.

CHAPTER 6
Bill Denver/Equi-Photo, 60; Kendra Bond, 66; Cheryl Manista, 66, 67; EquiPix, 67; Karen Briggs, 68, 69, 70, 71; Anne M. Eberhardt. 69; CLiX, 70, 72.

CHAPTER 7
CLiX Photography, 84.

CHAPTER 8
CLiX Photography, 100, 101; Karen Briggs, 102, 105.

CHAPTER 9
Anne M. Eberhardt, 112, 119; CLiX Photography, 114.

CHAPTER 10
Anne M. Eberhardt, 132, 133.

(Tables in Chapters 2, 3, 4, 7, 8, 9, and 10 excerpted from *Feeding and Care of the Horse*, second edition, by Lon D. Lewis, DVM, PhD, Diplomate, American College of Veterinary Nutrition, Topeka, Kansas.
Williams & Wilkins, 1996, Baltimore, Philadelphia, etc. A Waverly Company.

COVER/BOOK DESIGN — SUZANNE C. DEPP
COVER PHOTO—THE BLOOD-HORSE PUBLICATIONS

# About the Author

Karen Briggs, B.Sc., is a career horsewoman who began riding at the age of eight and didn't, as her parents had hoped, "grow out of it." As an equine nutritionist and horse feed specialist for United Cooperatives of Ontario, a large feed company, she was

**Karen Briggs**

responsible for researching, designing, and marketing a new line of premium quality feeds for performance, pleasure, and breeding horses, and for providing common-sense nutritional information and ration balancing to customers across the province of Ontario.

She is also a Canadian Equestrian Federation certified riding instructor, and has managed farms and riding schools in both Canada and Bermuda.

Over the past 20 years, Karen has worked at both Standardbred and Thoroughbred racing stables, and competed in disciplines as diverse as Western pleasure, competitive trail, and dressage. She currently concentrates on three-day eventing, and provides nutritional advice on a consulting basis, as well as writing for more than 20 American, Canadian, and European equine magazines. She is a frequent contributor to *The Horse: Your Guide To Equine Health Care*.